SAGE Publications
London • Thousand Oaks • New Delhi

in association with

TheOpen
University

DOING CULTURAL STUDIES
The Story of the Sony Walkman

*Paul du Gay, Stuart Hall, Linda Janes, Hugh Mackay
and Keith Negus*

The Open University, Walton Hall, Milton Keynes MK7 6AA

© The Open University 1997

First published in 1997

SAGE Publications Ltd
6 Bonhill Street
London EC2A 4PU

SAGE Publications Inc.
2455 Teller Road
Thousand Oaks
California 91320

SAGE Publications India Pvt Ltd
32, M-Block Market
Greater Kailash - I
New Delhi 110 048

British Library Cataloguing in Publication data

A catalogue record for this book is available from The British Library.

ISBN 0 7619 5401 5 (cased)

ISBN 0 7619 5402 3 (pbk)

Library of Congress catalog card number is available.

Edited, designed and typeset by The Open University.

Index compiled by Isobel McLean.

Printed and bound in Great Britain by
BPC Consumer Books Ltd
A member of
The British Printing Company Ltd

CONTENTS

Acknowledgements

We should like to record our thanks to the following for their help while writing this book:

At the Sony Corporation, Tokyo:

Mr K Ohsone

Mr A Ogihara

Mr S Takashino

Mr J Shimoyamada

and (not now linked to Sony)

Mr H Kato

Mr S Ueyama

Mr Y Kuroki

and

Andrew Dewdney, Head of Film and Photography, and students of the Documentary Photography Department at Newport College of Art and Design, Gwent College of Higher Education.

These days it seems increasingly difficult to get away from 'culture'. Once associated almost exclusively with the 'arts', the term now pops up in the most unlikely of places. In that seemingly most 'material' of domains – the world of business and the economic – for example, 'culture' has come to occupy an increasingly important position. Over the last few years people working in large enterprises are likely to have found themselves exposed to 'culture change' programmes as part of managerial attempts to make organizations more efficient, effective and profitable. Similarly, in the political domain questions of 'culture' have achieved a remarkable centrality in recent times. Throughout the 1980s Margaret Thatcher's radical programme of reform was represented in large part as a cultural crusade, concerned with the attitudes, values and forms of self-understanding embedded in both individual and institutional activities. The Conservative party's political project of reconstruction was simultaneously defined as one of cultural reconstruction, as an attempt to transform Britain into an 'enterprise culture'. During the 1990s questions of culture have continued to dominate political debate but with a rather different inflection: this time the effects on national cultural identity of closer ties with the European Community have topped the political agenda.

In addition to the economy and the polity, the academy has also witnessed a massive upsurge of interest in things cultural. In universities and colleges throughout the land, a subject called 'cultural studies' has emerged as higher education's most upwardly mobile discipline. A brief glance at contemporary higher education curricula reveals its onward march with courses in semiotics appearing in management schools, and seminars on television and popular culture developing in sites stretching from sociology to modern languages and literature.

There are many reasons for this explosion of 'culture', but two in particular stand out. The first we might call *substantive* (i.e. concerned with matters of empirical substance), in that it refers directly to the increased importance of cultural practices and institutions in every area of our social lives. The growth of the mass media, new global information systems and flows, and new visual forms of communication have had – and continue to have – a profound impact on the ways our lives are organized and on the ways in which we comprehend and relate to one another and to ourselves. The second we might term *epistemological*, in that it is primarily concerned with matters of knowledge.

Within the explanatory hierarchy of the social sciences in general and sociology in particular, culture has traditionally been allotted a rather inferior role. In contrast to economic and political processes, for example, which were routinely assumed to alter material conditions in the 'real' world – how people thought and acted – in ways which could be clearly identified and described, and hence to provide 'hard' knowledge of the social world, cultural processes were deemed rather ephemeral and superficial. Because cultural processes dealt with seemingly less tangible things – signs, images, language, beliefs – they were often assumed, particularly by Marxist theorists, to be 'superstructural', being both dependent upon and reflective of the primary status of the material base and thus unlikely to provide social scientists with valid, 'real' knowledge.

In recent years all this has changed and the cultural has come to occupy a much enhanced position in the social sciences. Rather than being seen as merely reflective of other processes – economic or political – culture is now regarded as being as constitutive of the social world as economic or political processes. Not only this, in recent years 'culture' has been promoted to an altogether more important role as theorists have begun to argue that because all social practices are meaningful practices, they are all fundamentally cultural. In order to conduct a social practice we need to give it a certain meaning, have a conception of it, be able to think meaningfully about it. The production of social meanings is therefore a necessary precondition for the functioning of all social practices and an account of the cultural conditions of social practices must form part of the sociological explanation of how they work. Cultural description and analysis is therefore increasingly crucial to the production of sociological knowledge.

The aim of this book is to introduce you to both these strands of the contemporary turn to culture – the substantive and the epistemological – and to do so through the medium of a particular case-study: that of the Sony Walkman[*]. Through the Walkman example we hope to show you not only how and why cultural practices and institutions have come to play such a crucial role in our lives in the present, but also to introduce you to some of the central ideas, concepts and methods of analysis involved in doing a 'cultural study'.

We have chosen the Walkman because it is a typical cultural artefact and medium of modern culture, and through studying its 'story' or 'biography' one can learn a great deal about the ways in which culture works in late-modern societies such as our own. In examining the production of cultural artefacts in the contemporary world, for example, sociologists increasingly focus upon the activities of a relatively small band of transnational corporations such as Disney Corporation, News International and Sony. For it is huge business corporations such as Sony which produce many of the products we routinely employ in our everyday cultural lives – whether they be videos, music cassettes and CDs or other forms of cultural software such as computer games, as well as the hardware, such as the Walkman or PlayStation, on which to run them. To explore how culture works in the present day therefore requires us to focus our attention on the structure, strategy and culture of these increasingly global commercial enterprises.

* Sony and Walkman are registered trademarks of the Sony Corporation.

In the past it was not unusual for sociological analyses of cultural products to begin and end with these processes of production. The mode of production of a cultural artefact was assumed to be the prime determinant of the meaning which that product would or could come to possess. This book breaks with this logic in that it analyses the biography of a cultural artefact in terms of a theoretical model based on the **articulation** of a number of distinct processes whose interaction can and does lead to variable and contingent outcomes. By the term 'articulation' we are referring to the process of connecting disparate elements together to form a temporary unity. An 'articulation' is thus the form of the connection that can make a unity of two or more different or distinct elements, under certain conditions. It is a linkage which is not necessary, determined, or absolute and essential for all time; rather it is a linkage whose conditions of existence or emergence need to be located in the contingencies of circumstance (see Hall, 1996). Thus, rather than privileging one single phenomenon – such as the process of production – in explaining the meaning that an artefact comes to possess, it is argued in this book that it is in a combination of processes – in their articulation – that the beginnings of an explanation can be found.

The five major cultural processes which the book identifies are: *Representation, Identity, Production, Consumption* and *Regulation*. These five processes form the basis of the sections of this book. Taken together, they complete a sort of circuit – what we term the **circuit of culture** – through which any analysis of a cultural text or artefact must pass if it is to be adequately studied (a similar approach has been developed by the cultural theorist Richard Johnson, 1986). As we argue in this book, to study the Walkman culturally one should at least explore how it is represented, what social identities are associated with it, how it is produced and consumed, and what mechanisms regulate its distribution and use.

articulation

circuit of culture

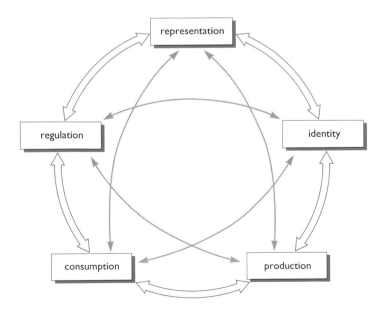

The circuit of culture

Remember that this is a circuit. It does not much matter where on the circuit you start, as you have to go the whole way round before your study is complete. What is more, each part of the circuit is taken up and reappears in the next part. So, having started with *Representation*, representations become an element in the next part, that is, of how *Identities* are constructed. And so on. We have separated these parts of the circuit into distinct sections but in the real world they continually overlap and intertwine in complex and contingent ways. However, they are the elements which taken together are what we mean by doing a 'cultural study' of a particular object.

Doing Cultural Studies: the story of the Sony Walkman is divided into six sections that directly mirror, in miniature, the structure or sequence of the series – *Culture, Media and Identities* – as a whole. Thus in section 1 we begin with questions of meaning, and indicate that meaning does not arise directly from an object, 'the thing in itself', but from the way in which an object – in this case the Walkman – is *represented* in language, both oral and visual. Here we are starting with the first of the key processes in our cultural circuit – with the establishment of cultural meaning through the practice of *representation*. Subsequently, in section 1.8, where the advertising 'discourse' surrounding the Walkman is analysed, we take this idea forward into the analysis of particular *representations* – the advertising texts which played such a crucial role in fixing the meaning and image of the Walkman. Section 1 is not solely concerned with representations, however. It also raises the question of how various groups and types of people came to be associated with the Walkman. In short, to questions of representation we add a second moment in our circuit – that of *Identities*.

Sections 2, 3 and 4 focus on the *Production* of the Walkman as a cultural artefact. Through the example of the Walkman it is shown how analysing the production of a cultural artefact in the present day involves not only understanding how that object is produced technically, but how that object is produced culturally; how it is made meaningful – what we term 'encoded' with particular meanings – during the production process. In thinking about the *production of culture*, then, we are also simultaneously thinking about the *culture of production* – the ways in which practices of production are inscribed with particular cultural meanings. This concern with the culture of production takes us back once again to questions of *representation* and *identity*, but also forward to questions of *consumption*.

Section 2 considers how the production of the Walkman was *represented* in distinct ways: as the activity of inspired individuals, as the result of the unique organizational culture of Sony and as a happy accident at work. We examine the ways in which the *identity* of Sony as a company was continually created and recreated through these different representations, extending the earlier discussion of individual and group identities to that of corporate identities.

Section 3 highlights the ways in which the Walkman was 'encoded' with certain meanings during its production process and how these were aimed at establishing an *identification* between object and particular groups of *consumers*. In particular, we focus upon the role of design in this process, exploring the ways in which designers attempt to bring together or 'articulate' two key moments in the cultural circuit – *production* and *consumption*.

Section 4 highlights Sony's ongoing attempts to become a 'global' entertainment corporation. In particular, it focuses upon the company's strategy of combining the production of cultural hardware – the Walkman and so on – with cultural software – the music that people play on their machines – to offer consumers a total 'cultural' package. Once again, we highlight the *articulation of production and consumption* that this strategy of 'media synergy' is designed to effect. We also point to the difficulties inherent in Sony's attempt to achieve such a close fit between production and consumption.

Section 5 explores processes and practices of cultural *Consumption*. As our notion of the 'cultural circuit' suggests, meaning-making is an ongoing process. It does not just end at a pre-ordained point. While producers attempt to encode products with particular meanings and associations, this is not the end of the story or 'biography' of a product, because this tells us nothing about what those products may come to mean for those using them. In other words, meanings are not just 'sent' by producers and 'received', passively, by consumers; rather meanings are actively made in consumption, through the use to which people put these products in their everyday lives.

Finally, section 6 explores some of the effects that Walkman use has had upon the *Regulation* of cultural life in modern societies. In this section, we locate the Walkman as one of the latest in a long line of technological innovations which has challenged traditional distinctions between public and private space. We examine the ways in which Walkman use breaks with established representations of public and private space and how its status as 'matter out of place' – being both public and private at the same time and hence *neither simply public nor simply private* – leads to attempts by institutions to regulate its usage. We also indicate some of the ways in which these problems of *cultural regulation* have come to the attention of Sony and how they have impacted on the *design and production* of the Walkman.

Paul du Gay

MAKING SENSE OF THE WALKMAN

1.1   Introduction

Do you own a 'personal stereo'? Do you know anyone who does? Even if you do not, I am sure you know what a Sony Walkman is and what it is used for. You have probably seen someone listening to one or pictures of people using one, in magazines, advertisements or on television. You may not know how the Sony Walkman actually works – to produce one requires a considerable degree of technological 'know-how'. Even putting the tapes in and turning the machine on may give you trouble to start with if you are not very technically minded. In fact, although it was first shown to the international press as recently as the summer of 1979, most people in Britain will know something about the Walkman, in a general sort of way. It has entered into, and made a considerable impact on, our culture. It has become part of our cultural universe.

ACTIVITY I

One way of knowing whether something has become 'part of our cultural universe' is to see whether you can interpret or 'read' it – whether you understand what it means, what it is 'saying'. Before reading further, try the following simple experiment.

Look at the photograph in Figure 1.1 which shows something happening. What can you tell us, in your own words, about this picture? What sort of person is the woman on the left and what is she doing? What do you make of the person on the right? Who might he be and why does he look so puzzled? They seem very different – how is that 'difference' established in the picture? What are these two people doing in the same picture – what do they have in common? What sort of lifestyles are depicted in the picture? What sort of mood or feeling does it conjure up? Compose a little story that sets the picture in context: what happened before and what do you think happens after the photograph?

This is the first-ever advertising image for the Sony Walkman, taken from a poster for the Tokyo launch in 1979. It seems to be carrying a rather complex 'message' – what do you think it is? Since the text is in Japanese, which I am sure very few of you can understand, how come you are able to 'de-code' the 'message'?

Now we can explore a little further the observation in the previous paragraph – that the Walkman is now 'part of our cultural universe'. It means that the Sony Walkman has become inscribed in our informal social knowledge – the 'what-everybody-knows' about the world – without consciously knowing where or when they first learned it. This kind of shared, taken-for-granted knowledge is an essential element in what we call 'culture'. Our heads are full of knowledge, ideas and images about society, how it works and what it means. Belonging to a culture provides us with access to such shared frameworks or 'maps' of meaning which we use to place and understand things, to 'make sense' of the world, to formulate ideas and to communicate

FIGURE 1.1
Bridging the difference: launching the Walkman, 1979.

or exchange ideas and meanings about it. The Walkman is now firmly located on those 'maps of meaning' which make up our cultural 'know-how'.

The Sony Walkman is not only part of our culture. It has a distinct 'culture' of its own. Around the Walkman there has developed a distinctive set of *meanings* and *practices*. The very word 'WALK-MAN' conjures up an image, or an idea – a concept – of the device. We can then use the concept to think about it, or use the word (or image or drawing or sculpture or whatever) as a sign or symbol which we can communicate about to other people in a variety of different contexts, even though we may never have owned or operated one. It belongs to our culture because we have constructed for it a little world of meaning; and this bringing of the object *into* meaning is what constitutes it as a *cultural artefact*. Meaning is thus intrinsic to our definition of **culture**.   culture
Meanings help us to interpret the world, to classify it in meaningful ways, to 'make sense' of things and events, including those which we have never seen or experienced in real life but which occur in films and novels, dreams and fantasies, as well as objects in the real world. You can play the actual Walkman but you cannot *think* with it, or *speak* or *write* with it. Meanings bridge the gap between the material world and the 'world' in which language, thinking and communication take place – the 'symbolic' world. They dissolve any fixed distinction between the so-called 'real world' and, for example, the world of the imagination with its 'small objects of desire' – like the Walkman or other consumer goods which we often fantasize about. We are perfectly capable of understanding such dreams, of interpreting their meaning, even if they only exist in the imagination.

It does not follow, of course, that all meanings are equally valid. But the distinction between a 'true' and a 'false' meaning is nowhere nearly so clear-cut as we suppose. It is easier to speak of those meanings which are widely shared and agreed upon within a culture, which carry a high degree of consensus at a particular time, compared with those which are held by only a few people. But even this is not a hard-and-fast distinction. Since our frameworks of meaning are constantly shifting, we can never be certain that what appears to be a marginal meaning at one time, will not become the dominant and preferred meaning at some later stage. And many readings, though perfectly plausible, may not be correct: how do you know, for example, that your way of reading the photograph is the one, true meaning? (We discuss this question of the 'multi-accentuality' of meaning and language at greater length below.)

So, the Walkman is 'cultural' because we have constituted it as a meaningful object. We can talk, think about and imagine it. It is also 'cultural' because it connects with a distinct set of *social practices* (like listening to music while travelling on the train or the underground, for example) which are specific to our culture or way of life. It is cultural because it is associated with certain *kinds of people* (young people, for example, or music-lovers); with certain *places* (the city, the open air, walking around a museum) – because it has been given or acquired a social profile or *identity*. It is also cultural because it frequently appears in and is represented within our visual languages and media of communication. Indeed, the *image* of the Sony Walkman – sleek, high-tech, functional in design, miniaturized – has become a sort of metaphor which stands for or represents a distinctively late-modern, technological culture or way of life. These meanings, practices, images and identities allow us to place, to situate, to decipher and to study the Walkman as a cultural artefact.

To study the Sony Walkman 'culturally' is therefore, in part, to use it as a clue to the study of modern culture in general. The Walkman gives us insights into the shared meanings and social practices – the distinctive ways of making sense and doings things – which are the basis of our culture. That is indeed the main purpose of this book – to set up an approach to the study of 'culture', using the Walkman as a case-study. Subsequently the analytic approach outlined in this case-study of the Walkman can be refined, expanded theoretically and applied to new objects of cultural study.

1.2   What is 'culture'?

It is time to offer a more developed definition of 'culture'. It is worth starting by acknowledging that this is a difficult concept, and we shall be continually refining this definition. Here we can only make a start on the process.

In *Keywords* (1976) the cultural theorist and critic, Raymond Williams, defined *culture* as one of the four or five key concepts in modern social knowledge. He reminded us that the term was originally associated with the idea of the tending or cultivation of crops and animals – as, for example, in *agri-culture* – from which we derive one of its central modern meanings: culture as the process of human development. During the Enlightenment, culture – and its synonym, 'civilization' – were used to describe the general, universal processes of human development and progress which – it was assumed – European civilization had achieved, in contrast with that of more 'rude', less civilized societies. In the nineteenth century, under the influence of the German writer, Herder, as well as the Romantic movement and the rise of nationalism, 'culture' came to be associated with 'the specific and variable cultures of different nations and peoples' – that is, it described the way of life of particular groups, peoples, nations or periods: a meaning which led to the word being more commonly used, as it often is today, in the plural – 'cultures'. It is this meaning which we still find active when the word 'culture' is used to refer to the particular and distinctive 'way of life' of a specific social group or period. In the latter half of the nineteenth century, following Matthew Arnold's famous book, *Culture and Anarchy*, the word 'culture' acquired a more restrictive meaning in English – referring now to a state of intellectual refinement associated with the arts, philosophy and learning. This meaning persists in the present day, when 'culture' is used to refer to the 'high arts', as compared with 'popular' culture (what ordinary folk, the relatively unsophisticated masses, do) or 'mass' culture (associated with the mass media and mass consumption).

You will find traces of all these meanings still active wherever the concept of 'culture' is used. However, the definition which is probably most relevant to how the concept is used here really emerges at the end of the nineteenth and through the twentieth centuries, and is associated with the rise of the human and social sciences. This definition emphasizes the relation of culture to *meaning*. Williams calls this the *social* definition of culture, 'in which culture is a description of a particular way of life which expresses certain meanings and values not only in art and learning but also in institutions and ordinary behaviour. The analysis of culture, from such a definition, is the clarification of the meanings and values implicit and explicit in particular ways of life, a particular "culture"' (Williams, 1961, p. 57). This is very close to those 'collective representations' which, in the sociological tradition, provided the shared understandings which bound individuals together in society. Collective representations, according to Emile Durkheim, one of sociology's founding figures, were social in origin and referred to the shared or common meanings, values and norms of particular peoples as expressed in their behaviour, rituals, institutions, myths, religious beliefs and art. This formed the basis of the anthropological study of so-called 'primitive' peoples.

Williams placed considerable emphasis on the close connection between culture, meaning and communication. 'Our description of our experience', he argued, 'comes to compose a network of relationships, and all our communication systems, including the arts, are literally parts of our social organization' (1961, p. 55). The process of exchanging meanings was the same as the building up of relationships and 'the long process of comparison and interaction is our vital associative life' (ibid.). For him, therefore, there was little or no distinction between studying 'the culture' and studying 'society'. He assumed that the cultural meanings and values of society would, broadly speaking, reflect, mirror and express its social and institutional relations: 'Since our way of seeing is literally our way of living, the process of *communication* is in fact the process of *community*: the offering, reception and comparison of new meanings, leading to the tensions and achievements of growth and change' (ibid.; emphasis added).

Subsequent developments in sociology and cultural studies have retained Williams' emphasis on the centrality to culture of the giving and taking of meaning, of communication and language. But they have questioned whether there is ever only one 'whole way of life' in complex societies, and stressed more that the process of the production and circulation of meaning needs to be studied *in its own terms*. How *is* meaning actually produced? Which meanings are shared within society, and by which groups? What other, counter meanings are circulating? What meanings are contested? How does the struggle between different sets of meanings reflect the play of power and the resistance to power in society? New developments have also placed more stress on the particular mechanisms by which meaning is produced and circulated – the forms of culture, as opposed to the content. And this, in turn, has directed attention to the communication process itself and the medium in which meaning is constructed – i.e. *language*. Is language simply a *reflection* of the social relations and institutions of society or is it in some ways *constitutive* of society? Recent theorists in social theory and cultural studies have put much greater stress on the centrality and the relative autonomy of culture. We cannot just 'read off' culture from society. We need to analyse the role of 'the symbolic' sphere in social life in its own terms – an emphasis which is not all that different from what Durkheim and the classical sociologists and anthropologists were arguing. This critique gives the production of meaning through language – what is sometimes called **signification** – a privileged place in the analysis of culture. All social practices, recent critics would argue, are organized through meanings – they are *signifying practices* and must therefore be studied by giving greater weight to their cultural dimension. (Many of these points are more fully developed in **Hall**[*], ed., 1997.)

signification

You will find these two meanings of the word 'culture' – culture as 'whole way of life' and culture as 'the production and circulation of meaning' – constitute a recurrent theme; and since the tensions and debates between them have not been resolved, we make no attempt to provide a final resolution. This remains one of the central arguments in sociology and cultural studies, about which, as you read further, you may develop your own views. However, one implication of all this is clear. Whether you take the view that culture and society are inextricably interwoven, or you believe that they are separate but related spheres (the connections between which are not automatic but have to be studied concretely in each instance), the result of this 'cultural turn' is to give culture a central place in the human and social sciences today and a significance which is very different from the rather subordinate position it used to have in conventional sociological theorizing.

1.3 Meanings and practices

Culture, then, is inextricably connected with the role of *meanings* in society. It is what enables us to 'make sense' of things. But how does this 'meaning-making' work? Partly, we give things meaning by the way we *represent* them, and the principal means of representation in culture is *language*. By language, we do not only mean language in the strict sense of written or spoken words. We mean *any* system of representation – photography, painting, speech, writing, imaging through technology, drawing – which allows us to use signs and symbols to represent or *re-present* whatever exists in the world in terms of a meaningful concept, image or idea. Language is the use of a set of signs or a signifying system to represent things and exchange meaning about them.

We can see this process of meaning-construction at work if we think of the moment in 1979 before what we now know as the Walkman existed. How

[*] A reference in bold type indicates another book, or chapter in another book, in the series.

were journalists able to 'make sense' of something they had never seen before? Just looking at the device would not help, for the machine could not speak or explain itself. It did not possess, and could not express, its own intrinsic meaning. Meaning is constructed – given, produced – through cultural practices; it is not simply 'found' in things.

One way of trying to fix its meaning was to use a familiar language to describe or 'represent' the device – and thus to bring it into discourse, into the orbit of meaning, to make it intelligible to us. The audio-editor of the magazine *Radio Electronics,* Larry Klein, describing this moment ten years later, uses both words and an image. He says that at the press conference in 1979, the manufacturers first showed journalists a 'smallish stereo-headphone cassette-player' (Klein, 1979, p. 72). Here Klein tries to use language in a plainly descriptive way to represent what the Walkman meant. However, Klein's description only works if you already know what such words as 'stereo', 'headphone' and 'cassette-player' mean. What he was really saying was: 'this object works *like* a small stereo-headphone cassette-player'. He was using words metaphorically.

This gives us an important clue as to how meanings work. We map new things in terms of, or by extension or analogy from, things we already know. Where, for example, did the meaning of a word like 'headphone' originally come from? That takes us back, perhaps, to the practice of people in crowded rooms listening to record players by headphone, and thus, in turn, perhaps to the early days of wireless. Each meaning leads us back to another meaning, in an infinite chain. And since we can always add new meanings or inflect old meanings in new ways, the chain of meaning has no obvious point where meaning began – no fixed point of origin – and no end. Every time you trace a meaning back to what preceded it – from 'headphone' to 'wireless', for example – it refers back to something which went before it. We seem to step from meaning to meaning along a chain of meanings which is without beginning or end. So, we represent the new by 'mapping' it to what we already know. Or we build meanings by giving old meanings new inflections ('a Walkman is rather like a stereo tape-deck – only *very small and more mobile*'). Or we contest meaning, by replacing an old meaning with a new one.

As well as being social animals, men and women are also *cultural* beings. And, as cultural beings, we are all, always, irrevocably, immersed in this 'sea of meanings', in this giving-and-taking of meaning which we call 'culture'. We use language and concepts to make sense of what is happening, even of events which may never have happened to us before, trying to 'figure out the world', to make it mean something. We can never get out of this 'circle' of meanings – and therefore, we can never be free of the culture which makes us interpretative beings. Things and events simply do not or will not or cannot make sense on their own. *We* seem to have to try to make sense of *them*. This is an important point. It suggests that cultural meanings do not arise *in* things but as a result of our social discourses and practices which construct the world meaningfully. There is no point turning to the thing itself, going straight to the 'real world', to sort out our meanings for us or to judge between 'right' and 'wrong' meanings. The Walkman had no meaning of itself. It is us who, through the process of using words and images to form concepts in our heads which *refer* to objects in the 'real world', construct meaning, who made the Walkman mean something.

1.4   Meaning by association: semantic networks

We need to think of this process of 'making sense' or producing meanings as stretching far beyond the literal meaning of words used, as we showed in the Klein example above. In fact, as we saw, there is nothing simple or obvious about literal meanings. They, too, work metaphorically. The difference is, as we have suggested, that over time some meanings acquire an obvious, descriptive status because they are widely accepted, and so come to be taken as 'literal', while other meanings appear more remote and metaphorical. Everybody would understand if you said, 'This is a portable cassette-player.' But, until it had gained wide acceptance, not everyone would have understood if you said, 'This is a Walkman.' So-called literal meanings are themselves only those metaphors which have acquired a broad consensual basis of agreement in a culture. There is nothing simple, obvious, literal or fixed about the connection between a small, portable tape-machine and the word 'Walkman'.

However, if we want to map the full range of meanings, associations and connotations which the Walkman has acquired over time in our culture, we have to move well beyond the so-called literal or descriptive meanings. Over the last two decades, the Sony Walkman has acquired a much richer set of meanings – what are called 'connotations' – than was captured in Klein's simple description. Its circle of reference and representation has expanded enormously. For example, it has come in our culture to stand for things that are high-tech, modern, typically 'Japanese'; it is associated with youth, entertainment and the world of recorded music and sound. Each of these

semantic networks   terms belongs to its own networks of meanings – its **semantic networks**. Each is associated with its own language or discourse, that is, its own 'way of talking' about the subject. There is a discourse of technology, of entertainment, of youth, even of 'Japanese-ness'. To connect the Walkman with these semantic networks or discursive formations is to bring new ranges of meaning to bear on our understanding of what the Walkman represents, culturally. We constantly draw on these wider connotations and discourses to make sense of an object, to expand or specify its meaning.

Let us take at random some of the characteristics listed above. The idea of 'high-tech' belongs to a particular discourse which is widely used nowadays to characterize anything which is the product of recent, cutting-edge technological developments. It conjures up an association for the Walkman with the world of advanced electronics, information technology and the leisure gadgetry revolution – associations very different from those, like 'low-tech' or 'sustainable technologies', which would have located it at the opposite end of the scale of meaning. Similarly, the idea of the Walkman as 'modern' carries another, related set of semantic associations. It signifies the Walkman as something up-to-date – the latest in leisure consumer goods, meant for fast urban living rather than reflective repose. Its 'private-listening-in-public-places' aspect triggers off many themes associated with late-modernity as a distinctive way of life: the lonely figure in the crowd, using the media to screen out the routines of boring, everyday life; the emphasis on mobility and choice; the self-sufficient individual wandering alone through the city landscape – the classic Walkman person seen so often in its advertisements, the urban nomad.

'Japanese' is not only drawn from the rich discourse of national cultural stereotypes (alongside 'British', 'American', 'Italian' or 'Chinese' – each of which would have given our image of the Walkman a very different inflection). 'Japanese' is also a discourse which represents the Walkman as the typical product of a particular *kind* of technological and corporate organization, associated with Japan's rapid post-war economic growth. It conjures up Japan's pre-eminence in advanced electronics, its highly effective global marketing of high-quality, precision consumer commodities produced with the latest technologies. It has associations with corporate firms like Sony, which are supposed to be run according to highly efficient, new-style management principles. These may be stereotypes (see the discussion in sections 2 and 3 below), but they help to construct for the Walkman an image very different from, say, British industry or corporate management. The discourse of 'youth', on the other hand, identifies the Walkman with a particular section of the market – with young people and youth culture – and therefore with the youth-led consumer industries, with fashion, street-style, sport and popular music (though we know that the Walkman is actually enjoyed by a much wider range of people). The discourse of 'entertainment' connects the product to the world of leisure and pleasure, and therefore, by association, with the world of popular music and the recording industries, which are at the centre of modern leisure. In all these examples, we can see how the meanings of the Walkman have been steadily built up, each discourse expanding our concept or idea of it by connecting it with another set of semantic networks.

Another way in which the meaning of the Walkman is constructed is by marking its *similarity to* and its *difference from* other things which are rather like it. This consolidates what we may think of as the Walkman's identity. Primarily, the Walkman is a machine for listening to recorded music. But so are a number of other modern electronic replay devices. The Walkman is *like* some of these other pieces of equipment – the tape-recorder, the hi-fi set, the compact disc player. But it is also *different from* them. It is listened to by one person only, is mobile and can be played, at top volume and with very fine technical sound quality in public (almost) without disturbing or being overheard by anyone else. This combination of *similarities* with other machines and *differences* from them gives the Walkman a definite and specific position. Like coordinates on a map or an A–Z, they enable us to pin-point it, to separate it from the others in our mind's eye, to give it its own, special, cultural meaning.

The Walkman, as such, means nothing in itself. One important way of establishing its meaning within language is by marking these relations of similarity and difference, which allow us to map its position precisely in relation to, as well as to differentiate it from, the other objects in the same field or set. To put the point more generally, we may say that, in language, meaning arises by plotting the relation between what something is and what it is not. It is hard to define 'night' except in relation to its opposite – 'day'. Another way of saying this is that meaning is *relational*. It is in the relation between 'night' and 'day' that meaning arises. If there were no differences between them, it would be hard to distinguish between them. *It is difference which signifies.* (This is a basic point about how meaning is constructed in language and its implications are much more fully explored in **Woodward**, ed., 1997.)

1.5   Signifying practices

What makes the Sony Walkman a part of our culture, we argued earlier, is not only the 'work' which has gone into constructing it meaningfully, but the *social practices* with which it has become associated. We *do* various things with the Walkman. We make use of it in certain ways and thus give it significance, meaning and value in cultural life. There are a whole set of wider practices associated with it which define what is culturally distinctive about the Walkman: like listening while travelling in a crowded train, on a bus or in an underground carriage; listening while waiting for something to happen or someone turn up; listening while doing something else – going for a walk or jogging. Also, more metaphorically, the very 'modern' practice of being in two places at once, or doing two different things at once: being in a typically crowded, noisy, urban space while also being tuned in, through your headphones, to the very different, imaginary space or soundscape in your head which develops in conjunction with the music you are listening to; completing a hum-drum chore whilst keeping track of the latest rock-music 'sounds' or operatic performances; or walking around a reverently silent museum or art gallery whilst, in your ear, an expert art historian is quietly giving you a personal lecture about the artistic history of the exhibits you are looking at. By situating the Walkman in these different practices, we appropriate it into our culture and expand its cultural meaning or value.

What is important is that, though these practices involve bodily and physical movements, it is not their physical or biological character which makes them culturally significant. Simply moving the hand to press the 'Start' button is not, in itself, culturally distinctive. What matters for *culture* is that these practices, too, are meaningful. They are organized, guided and framed by meaning. They are meaningful for the participants involved. We call them **signifying practices**. As onlookers, observing them, we are not puzzled by them because, unlike the proverbial visitor from Mars, we know how to interpret them – they are meaningful for us too. We do not say, 'Look at the funny thing that person is doing – using her thumb to press that little knob. What's she up to?' We are able to make sense of what the other person is doing by *de-coding* the meaning behind the action, by locating it within some interpretative framework which we and the person doing it share. It is shared meaning which makes the physical action 'cultural'. It is meaning that translates mere *behaviour* into a cultural – a *signifying* – practice.

signifying practices

This argument has acquired a new significance in recent years with the onset of the 'cultural turn' in the human and social sciences. It connects with certain aspects of the classical tradition in sociological thinking which tended, until recently, to be submerged by more positivistic types of theorizing. We have already noted, for example, the importance which Emile Durkheim gave to the idea of *collective representations*. According to him, these 'collective representations' arose from society itself and provided the shared understandings which created social solidarity, binding individuals into society. In *The Methodology of the Social Sciences*, another classical sociologist, Max Weber, distinguished between mere behaviour, like the instinctive jerk of a knee when tapped with a hammer, and social actions which are culturally significant. He called the latter, 'action relevant to meaning'. Sociology, he believed, was the study of those social practices which require interpretative understanding, which we must refer to our cultural understanding in order to make sense of. Even Karl Marx, who is usually thought of as emphasizing the material factors in social life over the symbolic, argued that the worst of architects was cleverer than the best of bees because the actions of bees are genetically programmed, whereas even bad architects must construct a model of a building in their heads before they can construct it in reality – i.e. the physical act of construction is always organized and framed by a conceptual or cultural model.

1.6 Contemporary soundscapes

So far, we have been focusing on the 'culture of the Walkman ' in a rather narrow sense – the complex of meanings and practices which have served to flesh out its meaning, its cultural significance. But the Walkman connects to our culture in a wider sense. It sustains certain meanings and practices which have become emblematic of – which seem to stand for or to represent – a distinctive 'way of life': the culture of late-modern, post-industrial societies like ours. These link it irrevocably with certain key themes of modern culture. These, too, have become part of the 'what the Walkman means', of how we make sense of it, of what it represents. Central to this is its connection to music.

We think of contemporary, late-modern culture as dominated by the *image*. Ours is pre-eminently a visual culture. We are assailed from every quarter by visual images – television, film, photography, images in newspapers, magazines, on hoardings and public buildings, posters, instructions, directional signs, flickering computer screens, traffic cameras and so on. Most of the examples of representation analysed in **Hall** (ed., 1997), for example, are visual. The impact of the visual is so overwhelming that we sometimes forget that it has been accompanied by a cultural revolution almost as ubiquitous. This is the revolution in *sound*. There have been extraordinary advances throughout the twentieth century in electronic recording and replay technology, leading to the widespread availability today of record-players and tape-recorders and a range of technically sophisticated stereo and CD equipment (see Negus, 1997).

Culturally, the rise of 'pop music' in the 1950s was a defining moment. It led to an enormous expansion of the popular music industry, with its turnover of millions, its key role in the production since then of the distinctive 'world' of rock music, and its dominating presence in radio and television. There is radio itself – more and more, in its local proliferation and its transistorized forms, a channel for music rather than speech. There is the whole ambience of youth culture, with its supporting industries in entertainment, fashion, sport and leisure activities, magazines and the image-creation, publishing, celebrity and public relations industries – much of it organized around or pervaded by popular music and its performers.

At the other end of the spectrum, there is the astonishing improvement in sound quality achieved for classical music and the recent spread in the popularity of opera. More and more activities of every kind and every sort of public space have been 'enhanced' by the addition of soothing piped or 'canned' music; there is the continuing vigour of local music-making as a cultural pursuit. If we can conjure up a picture of what 'modernity' is like as a distinctive way of life, with an image of, say, the Manhattan skyline or some other similar urban landscape – as many television programmes and films do – we could do the same by tuning in to the typical sounds of the late-modern city. They would include not only snatches of recorded music but other familiar sounds, like the wailing siren of ambulance, fire-engine or police car, the endless murmur of traffic, the exhalations from sooty exhausts, wheezing engines and chugging juggernauts – the modern soundscape.

soundscape

The concept of the **soundscape** is taken from Murray Schafer's book, *The Tuning of the World*, and the idea is elaborated by Iain Chambers, in his essay on the Walkman which is discussed at length below, in section 5 of this book. The all-pervasive character of music in contemporary urban culture is wittily captured by Nicolas Spice in his review in *The London Review of Books* of two books on recording and *muzak*:

> Around eleven o'clock on Monday morning, I phone Dell Computers to query an invoice, but the accounts department is engaged, so I get put through instead to the development section of the first movement of the

New World Symphony. The music I intrude on is intense and self-absorbed. I am like a child in a children's book who has stumbled through a gap in reality and fallen headlong into another world. I pick myself up and follow Dvorak's gangly, adolescent theme as it strides from instrument to instrument and key to key on its way home to the tonic. I think of it as healthy, wide-eyed and affirmative, trumpeting an ingenuous faith in energies which will lead to a new world far braver than any Dvorak might have imagined, the world of Dell Computers in Bracknell, of fax-modems, of the Internet, of telephones capable of pouring Dvorak's impassioned certainties into the ears of office workers on humdrum Monday mornings.

Into my mind drifts the image of Dvorak's head, moustachioed and visionary, gazing, a bit like the MGM lion, out of a locket-shaped gold-embossed medallion in the centre of the box which housed my LP of the *New World* Symphony when I was 12, a record whose brash appearance made me uneasy and slightly embarrassed. Reception interrupts my nostalgia to ask me if I want to go on holding (ah, if only I *could* let go!). When I mumble assent, I am returned to the symphony, where the mood has changed. It is the second movement now, and a cor anglais is singing above muted strings. This tender melody reminds me of a mawkish novel by Josef Skvorecky. The details elude me, but I fancy *Dvorak in Love* to have been a soft-focus, rural idyll, and I fall to imagining a red sun rising behind a field of gently rippling Bohemian corn, and, beyond it, a girl in a dirndl beckoning seductively. 'Good morning, Sales Ledger, this is Martine, how may I help you?' I have been put through.

Phone-hold music is a late, trivial but characteristic effect of the technical revolution which over the past century has transformed the way we encounter music. Until the development of the radio and the gramophone, people only heard music when they played it themselves or when they heard other people playing it. Music was bound by time and space. Now, music is everywhere, streaming through the interstices between the lumpy materials of life, filling the gaps in the continuum of human activity and contact, silting up in vast unchartable archives.

(Spice, 1995, pp. 3–6)

This twentieth-century soundscape is composed of actual sounds. But there is also a 'soundscape of the mind' in which music plays a key role. Music, like reading (another private pleasure which can be done in public, on trains or buses), has often offered a sort of inner landscape of feelings, emotions and associations to which we can retreat from the bustle and hassle of the 'real world', a sort of 'second world', adjacent to but separate from the everyday one. We can tune in, through music, to the imagination, or escape into ourselves, whether listening to recorded music in private or to live concerts or public performances. Gradually, this situation has been transformed by the revolution in recording and play-back technology. A succession of developments, from the portable transistor radio to the car stereo, has made it possible to transport this inner landscape of sound with one wherever one goes, simultaneously taking the pleasures of private listening into the very heart of the public world and the qualities of public performance into the privacy of the inner ear. The Walkman stands at the outer limit of this revolution in 'the culture of listening'. In section 5, in the context of a discussion of consumption patterns around the Walkman, we will look in some depth at the blurring of boundaries between the public and the private spheres which this quiet revolution has brought about.

Here, however, we want to highlight another, related, aspect. These new technologies of listening, as Iain Chambers and other writers point out, are highly responsive to personal choice. Of course, they are ultimately dependent on what does – and what does not – get recorded by the record companies. But the Walkman has taken its place alongside the range of new home-based sound recording and replay technologies, whose overall effect has been to maximize personal choice in listening. You can not only put together a selection from many musical genres and thus construct a medley of different moods and impressions, emotions and fantasies, a personal ensemble to suit your own tastes, but, with the help of the Walkman, you can 'sample' it right there in the most public of places, through the medium of the ear. As with the other technologies, you can fast-forward from track to track, selecting or rejecting, repeating, or varying the combinations and the volume according to personal inclination. With these new means of cultural production, then, the role of the producer and the so-called consumer of culture are becoming much more interchangeable. Consumption is becoming more of a personal act of 'production' in its own right.

1.7 Culture in the age of electronic reproduction

In earlier times, it was the uniqueness of the painting or work of art, or the enduring quality of a particular performance of a piece of music, which was unrepeatable, that gave it its claim to status as an authentic work of art. In the world of the Walkman, the CD and the cassette-recorder, it is infinite repeatability together with its variability that is most striking. The German critic, Walter Benjamin, in a classic early essay entitled 'The work of art in the age of mechanical reproduction' (1970), fastened onto this shift as a critical turning-point in the impact of the new technologies of cultural production on modern culture – the growth of what Benjamin called 'mechanical' (and we would now call 'electronic') reproduction. Their infinite repeatability, Benjamin argued, is one of the essential characteristics of the modern means of cultural production, like the movie camera, and (by analogy, though Benjamin did not talk about them) the tape-recorder, the vinyl record and the audio-cassette. The practice of electronic repeatability has been raised to the level of a new art form in contemporary popular music such as 'house' and 'rap' music, for example by 'sampling' (the practice of copying fragments of other people's tracks, quoting them and combining them with new riffs and verses to create a new composition).

READING A

You should now read the extract from 'The work of art in the age of mechanical reproduction' by Walter Benjamin, which is a foundation text for modern cultural studies. First read the notes on this reading below, then turn to the Selected Readings at the end of the book and study Reading A. When you have done so, return to the text below.

Benjamin's essay is one of the earliest to identify the revolutionary impact of the new technologies of mechanical reproduction in the twentieth century on the status of the 'work of art'. It is considered a classic in terms of beginning to define some of the key characteristics of modern artistic culture. Note that, in this essay, 'work of art' means visual work – painting, lithography, photography, film.

Benjamin is discussing the new techniques of mechanical reproduction which began to appear from about the 1870s onwards. What are the effects, he asks, on culture of this capacity to reproduce copies of works of art in large numbers and to circulate them far and wide throughout society?

He begins by setting the new technologies of reproduction in the historical context of earlier techniques. Then he notes the following consequences of the new capacity to 'mechanically reproduce' (try to follow these points through as you read):

1   Mechanical reproduction affects the uniqueness and 'authenticity' of the work of art.

2   It destroys its 'aura'. (What does Benjamin mean by this term?)

3   It shatters the tradition in which works of art were hitherto embedded.

4   It changes our sense-perception.

5   It replaces 'uniqueness and permanence' by 'transitoriness and reproducibility'.

6   It removes the work of art from the realm of ritual to that of politics.

Do you think that the effects of 'electronic reproduction' are similar?

So far, we have been discussing the Walkman in terms of the first concept in *Culture, Media and Identities*. However, Benjamin's essay and the discussion of new technologies of cultural production remind us that another reason why the Walkman has become so symbolic of developments in our wider culture is because it belongs to that long list of new media – the new technologies of producing, storing and circulating images and sound – which have transformed culture and communication over the last century. They include the telephone, wireless, radio, still and film cameras, television, the record-player and, more recently, the tape-recorder, transistor radio, audio- and video-cassette, the CD, the personal computer, photocopier, fax machine and mobile phone, to name only a few. Most of these are, most of the time, deployed for routine, everyday uses. Nevertheless, since they are both the sources and the channels for the circulation of meanings within the culture and since they both originate and reproduce sounds and/or images, it is correct to think of them as new sources of meanings and thus new means (i.e. *media*) for the cultural production/consumption of meaning. Objects of cultural meaning in themselves, they are also channels for *mediating* musical and visual meanings to a global public. Where, formerly, we depended on drawing, painting, the written and spoken word, letters and documents transported from one place to another, and books as the principal ways in which meanings were circulated throughout our culture and between cultures, now the scope, volume and variety of meanings, messages and images which can be transmitted (i.e. *media-ted*) have been vastly expanded by the harnessing of culture to the new electronic technologies. This has opened up a new frontier in modern cultural life and completely transformed the process of 'meaning-making' which, we have argued, is at the heart of culture. Meaning-making lies at the interface between culture and technology. (This story is taken up again in more detail in **du Gay**, ed., 1997.)

Throughout, you will find a close connection being drawn between *culture* and the *media*, between the meanings and practices which form the basis of all modern culture and the technological means – the media – by which much (though not all) of that culture is now produced, circulated, used or appropriated. No study of late-modern culture could afford to neglect – as an essential part of the study of the culture as a whole – the rapid development of new media. We include in this term the actual technologies, the corporate institutions (like Sony) which manufacture, sell and distribute – now on a global scale – both the 'means' and the 'meanings' which sustain the cultural process as well as their economic role and function. Today, the production and consumption on a global scale of 'cultural goods' represents one of the most important economic activities. In addition, each of these new **media**

media technologies **technologies** has a particular set of practices associated with it – a way of using them, a set of knowledges, or 'know-how', what is sometimes called a *social technology*. Each new technology, in other words, both sustains culture and produces or reproduces cultures. Each spawns, in turn, a little 'culture' of its own.

There are other connections between the Walkman and the culture of late-modernity. The best quality recorded sound once required a lot of heavy, rather cumbersome equipment. The Walkman, however, is eminently portable – convenient, lightweight, pocket-sized. (These issues of design are elaborated in section 3 below.) Like many consumer goods, the Walkman is designed to be worn, like one's clothes, as part of one's self-image or self-styling. Like the Lycra suit of the modern urban cyclist, it is virtually an extension of the skin. It is fitted, moulded, like so much else in modern consumer culture, to the body itself. Even the ear-pieces are now grooved to the shape of the ear, so that you have to look carefully to be sure a person is wearing them. It is designed for movement – for mobility, for people who are always out and about, for travelling light. It is part of the required equipment of the modern 'nomad' – the self-sufficient urban voyager, ready for all weathers and all circumstances and moving through the city within a self-enclosed, self-imposed bubble of sound. The Walkman is not only an essential part of this young person's survival kit; it is a testimony to the high value which the culture of late-modernity places on mobility. This mobility is both real and symbolic. The Walkman fits a world in which people are literally moving about more. But it is also designed for a world in which the social mobility of the individual with respect to his or her social group has also increased. The Walkman maximizes individual choice and flexibility. But there is some question as to whether it connects the individual to any wider social collectivity. Some critics argue that it insulates the person from the public, in his or her own radical individuality, and in this sense is typical of the more individualistic climate of the 1980s in which it established its popularity. Others – Chambers (1994), for example – argue that it is not as radically individualistic as it sometimes appears. This is a major debate, which is touched on again in section 5, alongside a more developed discussion about how the Walkman is shifting the boundaries between the public and the private spheres. However, before we leave this question of the Walkman's relation to the wider culture of its times, let us pause to set this aspect in a broader social context.

READING B

In his book, *Towards 2000,* Raymond Williams connects the rapid changes introduced by late-modern capitalist consumerism with the condition he calls 'mobile privatization'. Turn now to the Selected Readings at the end of the book and read the short extract from Williams' section on 'The culture of nations' from his book; it will help you to begin to reflect on the popularity and widespread use of the Walkman in the context of these broader cultural developments. When you have read it, return to the text below.

1.8 Walk-men and Walk-women: subjects and identities

So far, we have been exploring the relationship between culture and meaning. An object or concept like the Walkman takes on a range of cultural meanings, partly as a result of how it has been *represented* in visual and verbal forms. So one clue to the meaning of the Walkman lies in the study of how, throughout its short life, it has been represented. We turn next to this issue of **representation** as the practice of constructing meaning through the use of signs and language. (Representation is a major aspect of the different cultural processes which we are exploring; it is analysed at greater length in **Hall,** ed., 1997.) To refresh your memory, you will recall that, in discussing how meaning is produced in previous sections, we emphasized a number of representational strategies:

representation

1   The way in which existing meanings are extended from something we already know to something new, along what we called 'the chain of meaning'.

2   We also discussed the way the meanings of an object are expanded by associating it with different discourses or semantic networks.

3   We stressed the importance of marking the Walkman's *similarity to* and *difference from* other objects as yet another strategy for positioning or 'making sense' of it.

4   We highlighted the ways in which it acquired meaning by being articulated with a number of key themes in the culture of late-modernity (e.g. 'mobile privatization').

Now, by studying examples drawn from the language of advertising of and about the Walkman, you have an opportunity to analyse these representational practices and strategies in operation. Advertising, of course, is an economic as well as a representational practice. Its aim is to make people buy the product, to increase sales and thus maximize profits. But it is also a cultural practice because, in order to sell, it must first appeal; and in order to appeal, it must engage with the *meanings* which the product has accumulated and it must try to construct an *identification* between us – the consumers – and those meanings. Objects like the Walkman, as we said earlier, do not possess their own intrinsic meaning, and they cannot express their meaning for us. Advertising is the cultural language which speaks *on behalf of* the product. Advertising makes commodities speak. It must *address the buyer*. It must create an identification between the customer and the product. Somehow, it must get us to see ourselves as – identify with or acquire the identity of – a potential buyer of the product: the 'sort of person who buys and uses this kind of thing'. No matter how much we like and admire the people in the advertisements, if we cannot see or imagine ourselves in that role, we will often be more reluctant to shell out the money required to purchase the commodity.

Of course, we quite often buy things without seeing ourselves reflected in the people pictured in the advertisement. We buy them because we need them. But very few consumer choices are entirely rational and instrumental. We can never be certain that we have not been influenced, even in a vague way, by the way the product and its typical consumer has been imagined. Of course, advertisers can get it wrong. Otherwise, we would be simply robots, entirely at their beck and call. Nevertheless, the fact is that the people represented in the advertisements are designed to represent the kinds of ideal target consumers which the advertisers and their clients think *are* or *might be* typical product-users. And, in so far as the advertisement 'works', it does so because somehow it gets us to *identify* ourselves with the types of people or situations depicted in the advertisements. It constructs us as typical 'subjects-for-the-product'. We become, in our mind's eye, typical 'Walk-men' and 'Walk-women'. Not literally, of course. Most of us do not actually think we could ride a racing bike at speed *and* listen to rap music on the headphones *and* smile at the camera all at the same time. But perhaps we dream of one day, with a little help from the product, becoming as fit, attractive and sporty as the person in the advertisements. The language of advertising – and representation in general – operates as much on fantasy and desire as it does on rational choices and so-called 'real' needs. The people in the advertisements are therefore not a realistic representation of ourselves but an *imaginary* one. That is, after all, where identification takes place – in one's head. So, the language of advertising attempts to create or construct identification with the image. It does so by addressing us through meanings and representations that are working, in part, in the imagination. In other words, they work by engaging with our idealized self-images and our unspoken desires.

Let us start by considering three advertisements, all relating to the point we made earlier about the link between the Walkman and national identities.

ACTIVITY 2

Look at the advertisement reproduced as Figure 1.2. You can see that it is for a Sony Walkman. The words help pin that down. What else does the advertisement 'say'? Most of it is in Japanese, so the majority of you will not be able to read the text. You can read the numbers, but you may have difficulty in deciding what they are referring to. Without access to what is written, what else can you find to say about it?

The Walkman, we said, represents a popular idea of something that is typically 'Japanese' – typical in terms of technical sophistication and 'know-how'. This advertisement shown in Figure 1.2 is from a Japanese lifestyle magazine. We may not be able to read the text, but we can see one thing. The advertisement emphasizes the Walkman's technical qualities (note the little

FIGURE 1.2
A Sony Walkman
– in any language.

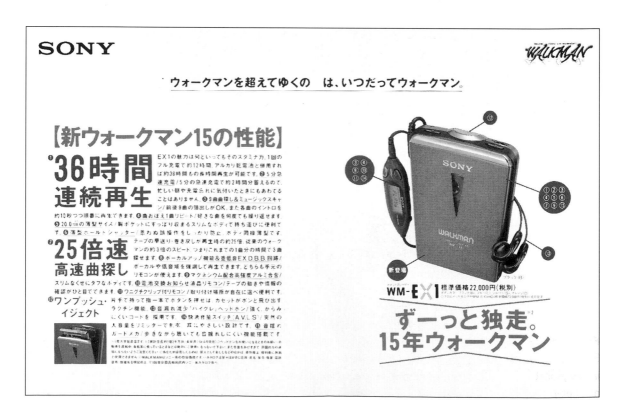

circles with numbered features, 1–15, and the corresponding numbers on the facing page). Made by a 'high-tech' company and represented and sold, here, on its 'high-tech' qualities – code-words for its 'Japanese-ness'. Isn't it interesting, then, that neither the name on the product nor when it appears in the text has been translated into Japanese (see the text at the bottom of facing page)? It is a Walkman in *any* language – the name itself has become a cultural value. It is the idea of 'Japanese technology' that has become its selling-point, its privileged meaning.

The same meaning is privileged in Figure 1.3, where the Walkman is being compared with the new Sony mobile phone – both of them sharing what is commonly believed to be another 'typically Japanese' technological

FIGURE 1.3

Small is beautiful: in the global market-place.

achievement – miniaturization. Sony personal stereos and mobile phones, like their people and their Bonsai trees, are, as the advertisement says, 'diminutive', and this is widely believed to be a Japanese characteristic. However, the use of the English word, Walkman, reminds us that, although the Walkman is the product of Japanese technology and management, its appearance is as global product – and the language of global consumerism is, of course, English (or, actually, American).

ACTIVITY 3

Now compare these advertisements, which work by identification with the technical qualities of the product (no people are represented at all in the advertisements: the 'subject' is the advanced technology and its 'Japaneseness'), with the next two advertisements in Figures 1.4 and 1.5, which are also addressed to non-English-speaking consumers (in this case, Italian). What do you think is being appealed to here? Which social identities or national stereotypes are being represented and invoked?

The identification being struggled for here is *youth* – indeed, crazy, zany, scatty youth: a meaning emphasized by the play on words in the text – 'Walkmania' – and the qualities highlighted ('Righe, quadretti, colore ed effetti' – 'Stripes, squares, colour and effects'). Not much cool, elegant technology here. Same product, different meanings.

FIGURE 1.4

FIGURE 1.5

Sony Italia: going crazy with Walkmania.

The next two advertisements underline the point that the Walkman can have many meanings, only some of which will be foregrounded in any single advertisement. Compare, for example, Figures 1.6 and 1.7.

Before reading further, try to guess from the layout and design the sorts of publications in which these advertisements appeared. What do these advertisements appeal to?

FIGURE 1.6
Winning with the Walkman (*The Sun*, 11 September 1987).

FIGURE 1.7   Classic, original, essential.

In Figure 1.6 the Walkman is being advertised in a tabloid newspaper, in this case *The Sun*. Here, the meanings foregrounded are (1) the GT Turbo – small but powerful, (2) 'savings' ('save up to £5 on a Sony Walkman'), and (3) 'hundreds of exciting prizes'. The strong meaning-association here is between the Walkman and the car – speed, power and masculinity, echoed in the phrase 'Change up to a Walkman 33'. Compare the popular meanings (speed, power, excitement, a windfall) and the jumbled design for *The Sun* with the cool, expensive elegance of the layout of Figure 1.7, where the advertiser can afford to leave most of the ad-space blank – it is deliberately 'wasteful' and extravagant. The associative meaning here establishes an equivalence between the sleek, black lines of the Sony Walkman, the cool, black sophistication of the singer, Marvin Gaye, and the 'cool sound' of 1970s' soul music – a classic album which should be in everyone's collection. The meanings of the one (Marvin Gaye) surreptitiously slide down the 'chain of meaning' and enrich the other (the Walkman). This is an expensive display advertisement for a colour supplement or a lifestyle magazine. In Figure 1.7 the elegant sophistication is constructed through the discourse of '*race*' – the image or concept of 'black soul music'. But the same *meaning* can be constructed through a very different image. In Figure 1.8 it is constructed through the discourse of *gender and sex*. The layout of Figure 1.8 has the same lazy elegance as Figure 1.7, but the key point of identification is the beautiful, near-naked blonde, with, of course, her Walkman; and, reflected in the pool but not in fact standing behind her, is the male singer (a 'walk-man'?) serenading her with a guitar. This photographic trick is really a metaphor because – of course – the singer is not actually there. He is coming to her, with the hint of romance if not the promise of sex itself, *through her headphones!*

Figure 1.9 is directed at the key cultural value of choice and difference. On the inside of the model's coat are suspended ten variations on the basic Walkman, illustrating the plurality of choices which the manufacturer has made available. The advertisement seems to suggest the idea that, amidst all this technological diversity, there *must* be one which is the perfect choice for *you* (struggling for identification). This is the late-modern consumer's dream – that though he or she will have the seal of fashionable approval by purchasing what everyone who has a personal stereo wants – a Walkman – this can be combined by tailoring your purchase to fit exactly the personal requirements of each individual user. This is getting the best of all possible worlds – mass marketing *and* personal differentiation. It attracts the bright, young, market-oriented consumer who wants both to consume in a global market and to express individual choice. It is, of course, made possible by new styles of production, based on multiple variations on a basic design, and also on the revolution in global marketing, which has moved on from selling the same goods to very large mass markets to selling in an increasingly differentiated set of 'niche' markets. The advertisement, however, does not speak of such production and marketing strategies. It foregrounds the casual, style-driven meanings with which the young consumer is likely to identify – the expansion of personal choice and the use of the market to express

Figure 1.8
California dreaming
… (*Sunday Times*
colour magazine,
7 December 1980).

individuality. Other Sony advertisements do exactly the same thing that Figure 1.9 does with products, only with people. The same basic product – the Walkman – is used by a wide range of *different types of people*. Choice and diversity through the market. Metaphorically, Figure 1.9 says, 'Whatever style suits you, the Walkman can provide'. Other examples which associate a Walkman with a range of different ages, genders, national identities and lifestyle groups within the same advertisement, seem to be saying, 'Whoever you are, the Walkman can satisfy'.

Figure 1.9
Spoilt for choice.

We emphasized earlier the theme of mobility. Many of the Walkman advertisements pick this up through association with the activity of *walking* and thus, by analogy through the metaphor of *shoes*. One advertisement simply juxtaposed the Sony Walkman with three different pairs of shoes: the message was then anchored by the text – 'Why man learned to walk'. In other Walkman advertisements on the same theme, the metaphor of walking is broadened out to cover certain 'lifestyles' and 'social identities' which represent or embody the cultural idea of mobility, mobile privatization, portability and movement. Figure 1.10, for example, is from a series of advertisements, in which heavily used footwear of various kinds is converted, by collage and the addition of accessories, into a face.

ACTIVITY 5

The advertisement in Figure 1.10 is rather abstract in design. Can you identify any *social* characteristics in it?

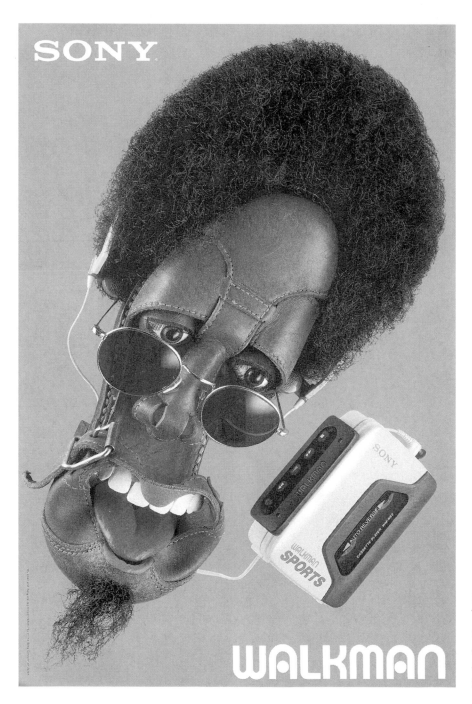

FIGURE 1.10
These boots are made for walking: one of a poster campaign for Sony (UK) Ltd.

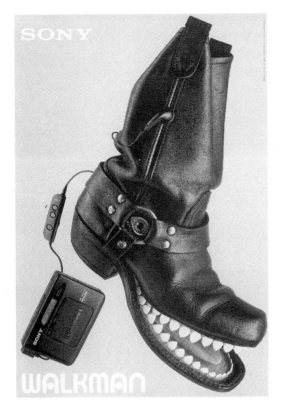

FIGURE 1.11

The particular example has strong evocations of black youth – the drawing, with its Afro hair-cut, goatee beard and dark glasses, is masculine and racialized, but drawn in a wild-youthful rather than a threatening way, picking up on the meanings associated with black street-style and its connotations of activity, movement, sports gear and 'hanging out' around city streets, rather than, say, more frightening associations such as 'mugging' (Concept: 'target the youth market'). There are other Walkman advertisements which thematize 'walking', showing only women's legs and shoes. But this truncated reference is enough to implicate a very different kind and class of 'subject' – female not male, with very fashionable high-heeled shoes and carefully groomed legs, fixed in that forward strut only achieved by high-fashion models on the cat-walk.

The next selection – Figures 1.11, 1.12 and 1.13 – belong to the same series as the baseball-capped youth, and sustain the youth–walking–movement–jokey complex of meanings. Here, no actual

FIGURE 1.12

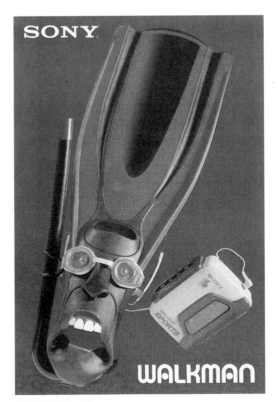

FIGURE 1.13

'people' have been represented. The faces have been wittily inscribed by addition, literally making the 'walking' shoe and the idea of the Walkman synonymous: the swimming flipper has become a face with goggle eyes and buck teeth; the boot has sprung a mouthful of teeth ('These boots are made for walk-*man*-ing'); and the tennis shoe sports a headband and has sprouted hair. All, of course, juxtaposed with a sleek personal cassette-player and the simple words, 'Sony Walkman'. These advertisements have enough personalized features to be 'recognizable' as invoking social identities, but are too abstract and deliberately constructed to be aimed at winning personal identification. They connect through their wit, their scale (enormous – this was a poster campaign) and their *leading idea*. They are conceptual advertising. They succeed by winning the play of ideas.

However, there are many other advertisements which do represent the idea of the Walkman through representing specific social identities. The bike-girl in Figure 1.14, on her racer, with low handle-bars and full cycling gear, blonde hair flowing, and the girl skater in Figure 1.15, also in summer shorts, on the

FIGURE 1.14 For the young and active.

Tuning In to Rappers

With phones on your ears and a cassette turned down low, you can have music wherever you go.

FIGURE 1.15

move, and blonde, and the skating couple, holding hands and moving at speed (Figure 1.16) – all neatly complemented by their Sony Walkman equipment – 'stress[es] the young and active', as the first picture caption says. It is interesting that, though gender aspects are strongly marked in all cases, women seem to be almost equally represented with men. What matters for the purposes of identification even more than gender is *lifestyle* and *generation*. The meanings cluster around youth, activity, sport, leisure, the outdoors, fitness, health, movement, getting-out-and-about. The machine

FIGURE 1.16
Off to a running start.

FIGURE 1.17
Just the two of us: the intimacy of a shared Walkman.

is specified in terms of social identities through 'lifestyle' scenes or scenarios: youth, the outdoors, activity, the sporty lifestyle. And, in the case of Figure 1.17, where two people listen to the same Walkman, *coupled*.

Are these in fact the only sorts of people who use or could use the Walkman? They are certainly not. The actual and potential range of users varies widely, both by social class and generation, lifestyle and cultural interest. The Walkman can be used as effectively to pass the time of day in old age as in youth, plays any kind of recorded music, and is as useful for informational purposes as for entertainment and leisure. It works as well sitting down as on the move. But the representational repertoire of the advertising, where it is not trading on the 'idea' and credibility-rating of the name of Sony Walkman itself and its technological sophistication and high quality, is relentlessly and overwhelmingly clustered around these meanings of mobility, sport, activity, leisure and youth, youth, youth.

Most people assume that this is because Sony's biggest market share, by far, comes from purchasers in the young generation, and so all the advertising is doing is giving a (fairly accurate) reflection of who in fact does purchase and use the Sony Walkman. Whilst there is some truth in that, it is too simple a way of understanding how representation works. It assumes that youth and youth culture and generational youth styles already have their fixed cultural and social identities, outside of and apart from the product and the advertising. In other words, the advertisements are simply *reflecting* the social world of real Walkman users. But remember what we said about identification working through language on the imaginary and on our desires. Something else is going on here as well. For, if the Walkman advertising is successful in forging an identification for itself with these groups and lifestyles, then after a time it comes to stand for or symbolize them, culturally. The Walkman becomes a metaphor, a signifier, of Youth. To *be* young, active and sporty and to have 'street cred', you need to be sporting a Sony Walkman. It is constructed as part of the identity of 'youth'. You can enter the group, identify yourself with the crowd, and take on the identity of the sophisticated young urban nomad by acquiring the Walkman and thereby acquiring the meanings and cultural characteristics which it represents.

Here, the language of advertising is not so much a reflection of cultural identities which are already formed, as *constructing* identities through representation, by representing them in a certain way. The advertisements suggest that, to signify that you are 'young', you must possess a Walkman. But the way representation works – through identification – also suggests the opposite. If you purchase a Walkman you can claim membership of that new, emergent identity – the Tribe of Youth. So the language of advertising, and the ways it works by attaching meanings to identities, suggests that representation is not so much about reflecting the identities we already have as telling us what sorts of identities we can *become* – and how.

1.9 Summary

Our aim in this first part of the Walkman story has been twofold. First, it has set up the 'story' of the Walkman as a sort of case-study in sociology and cultural studies. Secondly, it uses the Walkman as a device for trailing a number of the key ideas, concepts and methods of analysis of the field of study; we think you will find it easier if you are introduced to some of these key concepts and skills through a concrete example.

In the Introduction to this book we explained the choice of the Walkman because it is a typical cultural artefact and medium of modern culture and, through studying its 'story', one can learn a great deal about how culture works in a late-modern society like ours. You may have noticed, therefore, that in this first section, we have tried to relate the Walkman to the three key words 'Culture, Media and Identities' (the title of this series of volumes). We began in sections 1.1 to 1.4 by using the Walkman to say, in simple terms, what *Culture* is, what it means to say that the Walkman is part of our culture. It is a cultural object because it has been constructed through a range of meanings and practices. As the latest in a long line of new technologies, it has had a profound impact on our culture and relates to or embodies some central themes in late-modern culture. Then in sections 1.5 to 1.7 we raised the question of the Walkman as a medium or channel for the circulation of meaning and musical forms and so brought in the second element – *Media*. Finally, in section 1.8, we have been following through the question of who – what sorts of people or lifestyles – are typically associated with the Walkman. Who is represented as the Walkman's typical subjects? This touches the third element – the question of *Identities*. In short, we have used the three concepts in 'Culture, Media and Identities' as pegs on which to hang key dimensions of the Walkman as a cultural study.

Section 1.1 started with questions of meaning, arguing that meaning does not arise directly from the object, the 'thing in itself', but from the way in which the object is *represented* in language, in discourse and in the concepts and ideas in our heads, in knowledge. Here, we introduced the first of our key processes in what we called in the Introduction to this volume 'the circuit of culture' – the production of meaning through the practice of *Representation*. (This concept is followed up in much expanded and developed form in **Hall**, ed., 1997.)

In the analysis of advertising in section 1.8, we took this idea forward into the analysis of particular representations. We looked at a selection of advertising texts which have played an important role in fixing the image and meaning of the Walkman. We linked the analysis of advertisements with the question of how various individuals, social groups, types of people and lifestyles came to be represented by or associated with the Walkman. In short, to questions about *Representation*, we added that of *Identities*. *Identities* is the second element of the cultural circuit; you will find it discussed at much greater length in **Woodward** (ed., 1997). In section 2 we continue on our journey to explore the production of the Walkman as a cultural artefact.

THE PRODUCTION OF
THE SONY WALKMAN

2.1   Introduction: the many origins of an idea

Trying to understand the production of the Walkman does not involve simply recounting a story that takes us from inspiration in the design office, to manufacture in the assembly plant, through the persuasions of the sales staff and then on to the act of consumption on the street or in the shopping mall. Instead, it involves having to consider a number of different narratives and representations of the 'facts' that have become associated with this technology. The different stories begin – and are perhaps most acute – when we consider the contrasting accounts of the Walkman's origins. Before writing this book we collected and sifted through a large amount of material that had been written about the Walkman. In reading through this, we were immediately confronted by a variety of explanations for the origins of the Walkman.

For a number of commentators, it was Akio Morita, one of the founders of the Sony corporation who was the 'inventor' or the 'father' of the Walkman. Iain Chambers writes that the Walkman was 'based on an idea that came to Akio Morita, President of Sony, while … walking in New York' (1994, p. 49). Elsewhere we can read that Morita came up with the concept to relieve the boredom of trans-Atlantic air travel (Sparke, 1987) or after observing 'his children's frustration at not being able to listen to music while travelling' (Rafferty and Bannister, 1994, p. 38). Morita himself, however, recalled that the 'idea took shape' on the occasion when his colleague (and co-founder) Masaru Ibuka came into his office with one of Sony's 'portable stereo tape recorders and a pair of … standard size headphones' (Morita et al., 1987, p. 49). For another writer it was Ibuka himself – 'the real genius behind Sony' – who 'dreamed up' the Walkman (Schlender, 1992). Another Sony colleague, Yasuo Kuroki (1987), wrote in his memoirs that the origins of the Walkman could be traced to the activities of a young engineer who remodelled a small cassette-recorder and enjoyed listening to it in private. Yet, *The New York Times* once informed its readers that Kozo Ohsone was the 'man known within the company as the father of the Walkman' (Sanger, 1990, p. 61). In contrast, Kozo Ohsone himself (Sony, 1989) and former Sony colleague Shu Ueyama (1982) both recalled that the Walkman emerged from a more collective process in which the company was involved in a quite deliberate attempt to come up with ideas for new products. A similar story was recounted in *The Times*, which located 'Mr. Morita as part of a team looking for innovations' when he recognized the potential of the small personal stereo (Knight, 1992). For another writer, the Walkman sprang from a more mystical source, emanating from the way in which Sony was infused with the 'Japanese spirit' of 'reductionism' and guided by a philosophical belief that 'smaller is better' (Lee, 1982, p. 55). But, then again, according to Andreas Pavel, the idea did not come from Sony at all. Rather, Pavel himself invented and demonstrated the potential of such a device in 1977 when he patented a 'stereobelt' that was put together from hi-fi units in pockets that were connected to headphones. Pavel challenged Sony in court during 1992 but lost his case; the verdict was that the personal stereo was too broad a concept to have one patent 'owner' who had 'invented' the idea. (Pavel took his case to the Court of Appeal again in 1996 but once more was unsuccessful, and for the same reason.)

This last anecdote is revealing, for it indicates that even after months of deliberation and testimony from expert witnesses, a court of law could not decide whether one claim was more valid than another. The conclusion was that the concept was 'too broad', that it built on ideas that were already in circulation and that anyone might have come up with this particular technology (Narayan and Katz, 1993). From our perspective, this means that we have to try to make sense of a number of different **representations**. Far from simply being 'fictions', these different accounts provide an insight into the contested character of cultural production and indicate how the Walkman has not only accumulated different meanings in advertisements and amongst different groups of consumers (as discussed in section 1), but also amongst those who participated in its production.

representations

If you pause to think about the list of anecdotes that we have just cited, you will notice that most of them refer, in different ways, to the distinctive people, working practices and qualities of the Sony organization. What this immediately tells us is that in studying the Walkman we are not only dealing with the way in which a cultural artefact is represented (as a *thing* in advertisements and photographs), we are also dealing with how the *processes* that have produced that artefact have been represented. We need to think about how the various processes of production are understood and given meaning by being labelled and categorized in various ways ('innovative', 'Japanese', 'teamwork' and so on). To understand production processes we need to refer to more than the title of occupational roles (engineer, assembler, president) and definition of specific activities (welding, wiring, purchasing). What we need to try to understand are the distinctive practices used in the production of the Walkman and the way that such widespread practices are represented in terms of *specific* values, beliefs and patterns of working. What we may call the **culture of production** is an integral part of the company way of life that informs intra-organizational decisions and activities (such as staff recruitment policies, departmental organizational arrangements and general management strategies). But it also informs the perceptions of outside observers, including those of us writing this study. In approaching the production of the Walkman we need to understand the distinctive ways of life – the cultures – within which the Walkman came to be constituted as an idea and then manufactured and marketed in a particular way.

culture of
production

In reading this section you should therefore bear in mind that we are dealing with an organizational culture that has been represented in a number of ways and has been accorded different *identities*. One of the most conspicuous distinctions we shall come across concerns Sony's national characteristics. Some observers in Europe and the United States have written of Sony as a characteristically Japanese company. Yet Sony has often been treated with suspicion in Japan for adopting what is considered to be a 'cosmopolitan' or 'foreign' style of working. You will find similar ideas appearing when we move on to consider the design of the Walkman. For some writers, this product is quintessentially Japanese due to its small size and other aesthetic characteristics. For other commentators, it is but the latest in a series of similar sound technologies that have appeared from companies in Europe, the United States and Japan.

Throughout this section we shall be pointing out those things that make it hard to categorize Sony as a typically Japanese company. We shall lead you to an argument that Sony is something of a global hybrid – a company that works internationally and draws on, and attempts to bring together, different styles of working found around the world.

2.2   Cultures of production, contexts of innovation

We have already referred to a number of contrasting views of the origins of the same technology (the Walkman) and different perceptions of the identity of the same company (Sony). Such contrasts suggest that we need to consider very carefully the claims that are often made about a 'Sony way', that is, an exceptional way of organizing the design and production of new technologies. We also need to be wary of such a concept because (more than business commentators and academic researchers) Sony has frequently sought to *represent itself* to the world as a distinctive, idiosyncratic and unique company. Such representations are an integral part of the company's attempt to create and maintain a distinct organizational culture. But, they are also part of how the company sells its uniqueness to collaborators, investors and consumers. Sony's representations of itself are part of the way in which the company goes about its day-to-day business.

In this section, then, we shall consider *some* of the distinctive characteristics of Sony's culture of production. We will consider the individuals who established the company, the company's relationship to the United States and the company's 'Japanese' characteristics. We will then move on to consider some of the ways in which production is also driven by far more practical concerns and economic expediencies, particularly the desire to find consumers for the products that are being developed and produced.

2.2.1   Heroic individuals

Many of the accounts of both the success of Sony and the Walkman privilege the activities of one man – Akio Morita, frequently referred to as 'Japan's best-known international businessman' (Rafferty and Bannister, 1994). In many books and articles Morita often appears as a symbolic personification of the technology (Walkman), the company (Sony) and the nation (Japan). Morita is often represented (and, has represented himself) as an inspired individual who almost single-handedly 'built the company' and 'created' the Walkman.

FIGURE 2.1

Akio Morita: the 'father' of the Walkman?

Not only has Morita frequently been called the 'inventor' and the 'father' of the Walkman, the history of the company has often been presented in terms of Morita's own biography. The two biographies – Morita's and Sony's – often run together: from the company's humble origins in war-damaged Tokyo to the first Japanese corporation to have a prestigious office in New York and, shortly afterwards, to their growth into a 'global corporation'.

Central to this success story is our cultural artefact, the Walkman. When Morita was featured, the Walkman was usually not far away. For example, when he was knighted at the British embassy in Tokyo during October 1992, both *The Sun* and *The Daily Telegraph* newspapers used the same headline: 'Arise, Sir Sony Walkman'. Two years later, when Morita retired from his post as Chairman of the company, the press coverage again featured the personal stereo. A typical headline at the time was *The Guardian* newspaper's 'Mr Walkman Steps Down'. Morita became an index and symbol of the company and the technology. For some commentators, though, Morita's significance was even larger than this. With his carefully promoted international profile, Mr Morita had become a symbol of Japan's 'rise from a war-devastated country to the world's second largest economy' (Nakamoto, 1994, p. 13).

What we are dealing with here is a very specific way of representing the success of the Sony Walkman. This is an explanation that links the life of one individual with the biography of a company and an artefact. It is an approach to social life and history with which you are probably familiar and which you can frequently find in newspaper articles and television documentaries. It is a model of history and social change explained as the result of the talents and activities of great individuals. This is the Walkman story as a *narrative* of an individual life and a company. Narrative is a very commonly used way of making sense of people's lives and giving a logical sequence of meaning to their activities: we might narrate our life 'story' in relation to a particular occupation (or 'career'), amongst a particular group of friends, or we might arrange photographs into a narrative sequence in albums and tell stories of our own histories. The individual narrative, in the form of the biography, has become one of the most popular literary ways of making sense of the lives of famous people (whether pop stars, tennis players or politicians). Biographies are always at the top of the best-seller lists. Here we find a similar approach being used in the way that the Walkman story is narrated. But, this is just one way of making sense of the company and the appearance of the Walkman. As you have probably realized by now, our approach in this book is quite different. We seek to place such individual activities and 'inspirational' talent in a wider context of cultural processes.

Let us begin doing this by considering some details about how Akio Morita founded the company. He was born in 1921 into a wealthy family who had been running a business brewing saki and soy sauce since the seventeenth century. In May 1946 Morita set up the company that would eventually become Sony, although at this time it was called Tokyo Tsushin Kogyu Kabushiki Kasha (Tokyo Telecommunication Engineering). Starting with capital invested by his father, Morita formed the company with Masuru Ibuka (born 1909) with whom he had been working during the war on the design of new types of bombs. Whilst Morita adopted the role of publicity-conscious businessman, Ibuka – more of a scientist and 'inventor' – was often less publicly visible outside Japan.

Another figure who features prominently in the Sony and Walkman stories is Norio Ohga. Born in 1930 into a family who owned a lumber business, Ohga trained as a singer and musician. When Morita and Ibuka's company produced Japan's first reel-to-reel tape-recorder in 1950, Ohga was decidedly unimpressed by it. He wrote to Morita to say that, from a singer's and a musician's perspective, the recorder was of dubious quality. Interested in such a response, Morita followed up this correspondence and recruited Ohga as a part-time consultant. For a number of years Ohga engaged in his musical career whilst acting as a consultant for the company. Eventually, Ohga was persuaded to abandon his opera career and in 1959 joined Sony full-time as the director of the tape-recorder business. In 1961 he became the head of Sony's new Design Centre and was eventually appointed to run Sony's joint venture with CBS records during the 1970s. Finally, Ohga took over from Morita and became President of the company in 1982.

Hence, from the earliest days Morita was not simply 'building' the company alone. He was also not simply starting from 'scratch'. Although breaking with tradition (the eldest son usually took over the running of the family business), he was also drawing on experience, knowledge and capital that he had gained from his upbringing. Morita had grown up in a family whose wealth and status had provided him with an environment where he had constantly come into contact with products from outside Japan, particularly phonograph recordings and cars from the United States. As we shall see, the relationship between Japan and the United States is a central motif in the Sony and Walkman story.

2.2.2 Sony, Japan and the United States

An important theme to both the Sony narrative and to the Walkman story are the various connections that have been established – and tensions that have endured – between Japan and the United States. Morita and his colleagues had grown up with many technologies which had come to them from the US, but the opening of the company for business coincided with the immediate post-Second World War context. As part of the post-war settlement the United

States had imposed restrictions which prevented Japan from manufacturing weapons. The US occupied the country formally until 1952, although occupying forces did not leave the island of Okinawa until 1972. It is within such a historical context that post-war industrial manufacturing had resumed in Japan. An infrastructure that had been put in place for producing weapons and war machinery was rapidly converted for making consumer products. With much of Japan devastated by conventional bombing and two cities obliterated by nuclear weapons, Morita and Ibuka formed a company in war-scarred Tokyo for the production of consumer electronics. The presence of the US hung heavily over such an enterprise.

The US–Japan connection continued when, in 1947, members of staff at the Western Electric division of AT&T in the United States made the first transistorized electronic components. This was a small amplification device that used semi-conductors. Having developed this piece of equipment, AT&T's engineers thought that these devices were only really useful for hearing aids (Barnet and Cavanagh, 1994). Hence, through the US regulatory anti-trust system, licenses were granted to the small Japanese company who wished to acquire the rights. The fee charged was a $25,000 advance against future royalties (ibid.). In order to arrange for the acquisition of the rights to the transistor, Ibuka and Morita began travelling back and forth to the US. Ibuka visited the US in 1952 to negotiate the deal and Morita returned the following year to complete and finalize the arrangements.

Having purchased the rights to the transistor, the company set to work on them and within two years the newly named Sony company had demonstrated that these transistors did indeed have more applications than their use for producing hearing-aids. The company had taken a technology that had been developed for a specific set of applications in the United States and re-used it in Tokyo to create something quite different to that envisaged by the engineers at AT&T: the first transistor radio.

READING C

You should turn now to the Selected Readings located at the end of the book and read 'Scratching a global dream' by Nick Lyons. This is a short extract from a journalistic account of the Sony story published in 1976.

This extract gives a sense of the position that Akio Morita occupied as a Japanese businessman in the 1950s. It gives you an idea of how Morita was travelling to the United States and Europe in order to acquire knowledge and learn about the international prospects for his company. Note how in this short extract Morita recalls realizing that in order to conduct 'global' business, a knowledge of the English language was vital. It is with such considerations in mind that a significant step was taken in changing the company's profile through the adoption of a new name. Here again we come to the way in which the company was representing itself and attempting to communicate its identity through the adoption of a specific company name.

Morita's and Ibuka's visits to the United States had convinced them that the
company required a more concise, memorable and less Japanese-sounding
title than Tokyo Tsushin Kogyu Kabushiki Kasha. The new title of 'Sony' was
originally to be the name for the transistor radio, but it was decided to use it
instead as the company name. It was very deliberately chosen. 'Sony' was
derived from the Latin word *sonus* meaning sound, but it was also close to the
American phrase 'sonny boy' which had become a slang term in Japan. It was
also chosen partly because it was perceived as 'placeless', or, to put it in
another way, global; importantly, it could be pronounced the same in many
different languages. As Morita recalled in his biography: 'The new name
had the advantage of not meaning anything but "Sony" in any language; it
was easy to remember' (1987, p. 70). The word Sony (unlike Matsushita,
Fujisankei or Toshiba, for example) was chosen because it was an un-Japanese
sounding name. It was a signal that Sony wanted to be more than a 'Japanese'
company.

2.2.3   Sony: signifying 'Japan'?

One of the most frequent ways in which companies and individuals are
referred to during everyday discussions is through the discourse of national
identity – the idea that people and things from and within specific national
borders possess very particular, idiosyncratic, national characteristics. When
attempting to make sense of practices or sounds and images from other places
in the world, one of the most common tactics is to attribute an identity in
terms of national distinctiveness. In this way, Sony has frequently been
written of as distinctively 'Japanese'. For example, when a reporter for *Arena*
magazine visited Sony's headquarters in Tokyo in 1988, he reported that:

> Every cliché you have ever been told about Japanese factories is here: the
> exchange of outdoor shoes for anti-dust plastic slippers; the line-up of
> bowing executives in reception; the sudden breaks in production for
> communal music-accompanied exercises and the ubiquitous posters and
> signs for 'zd' ... a reminder of Sony's platonic ideal of quality control: Zero
> Defects.
>
> (Taylor, 1988, p. 124)

Sony has sometimes been written of in such a way as a 'typical Japanese
company'. A number of peculiar characteristics have usually been identified
by those writers who have attributed particular attributes to Japanese
companies.

First, there is the notion of a strict hierarchy. This is a hierarchy of
occupations, whereby certain jobs (design) are more important than others
(assembling).

Secondly, there are certain idiosyncratic Japanese rituals. Journalists often
report that Japanese company life is visible in Sony – due to the way that

everyone wears the company's tan uniform – and it is audible – heard when company staff recite Ibuka's company poem 'Sony Spirit'.

Thirdly, for many years employees in Japan had a job for life with one company. In return, the employee would regard the company with loyalty and commitment beyond any formally drawn up contract of employment.

Fourthly, corporate life in Japan is shaped by a series of relationships between big cartels. For many years business in Japan was conducted within a context where competition was counterbalanced by a solidarity established by the six *keiretsu*. These were family-run trading companies which controlled business in Japan through a system of interlocking relationships that would occasionally provide mutual support.

It is on this latter point in particular, however, that the notion that Sony is a typically Japanese company begins to break down. These old *keiretsu* networks had been established since before the Second World War. Sony was a newer and smaller company and was not integrated into these structured business relationships and obligations. As a result, the company began to adopt slightly different working practices and was in turn 'viewed with suspicion' by those in the older Japanese companies (Sanger, 1990). Despite having a basic hierarchical company structure that was similar to other Japanese firms, Sony adopted different ways of working within this hierarchy (Schlender, 1992). One aspect of Sony's distinctiveness was its approach to recruiting and then placing staff within the company.

Like all Japanese electronics companies, Sony has for years regularly recruited technicians and qualified engineers from the universities. But the company has also made a habit of recruiting staff from competitors, a practice that at one time was considered a breach of business etiquette in Japan. In addition, from its earliest days the company developed a propensity for a risk-taking approach by recruiting 'bright eccentrics' (Barnet and Cavanagh, 1994). In doing this, Sony developed an approach that involved balancing the work of trained specialists with the activities of people referred to in Japanese as *neaka*. This term combines two Japanese words: *ne* meaning bright, cheerful and inspirational and *aka* which means optimistic, consistent and approachable. The aim was to locate open-minded people, willing to be moved around the company and acquire and utilize different experiences and knowledge.

In doing this, Sony was attempting to add flexibility (movement, new ideas, new experiences for staff) to a relatively inflexible system (hierarchical, life-time employment); it was a way of trying to add a creative impetus to a potentially rigid system. Company executive Kozo Ohsone explained it in the following terms: 'If you want to lower the cost of an existing product or find a better way to manufacture it, you assign it to experienced engineers who like what they are doing. If you are designing something new that is higher priced, with lots of features, you give it to the rookies' (quoted in Schlender, 1992, p. 25).

Such a comment, from a senior member of Sony management, gives an indication of how the company's employment strategy was directly informed by a consideration of the type of products that they were making. The company was aware of trying to combine the contrasting working practices that are necessary to produce these products. This involved bringing together a controlled, hierarchical and cost-effective managerial structure with mechanisms that allowed for idiosyncrasies, and encouraging ideas to filter up from below as well as directing from above.

When Sony were working on the Walkman, then, they were not simply and straightforwardly 'Japanese'. As the company itself put it, in one of their own publications on the Walkman, 'Sony operates both as a traditional Japanese company, managing from the bottom up through group consensus, and as an American company from the top down, by delegating responsibility to small design teams' (Sony, 1989, p. 14).

Such management strategies indicate that Sony had been attempting to develop a distinctive *culture of production*. This was a *hybrid* way of organizing work which drew from the conventions of business practice as developed in both Japan and the United States. It is important, then, that Sony is not categorized simply as a 'Japanese company'. They have rarely – if at all – been held up as an example of how North American and European companies should reorganize in the same way that motor manufacturers such as Toyota and Nissan have. And, it is worth noting that even when such companies have been identified as quintessentially Japanese, a degree of caution is required when assessing such claims. As Elger and Smith have noted, 'the rhetoric of Japanization ... often owes little to established Japanese ways of working' (1994, p. 6). Our point here is that Japanese companies have not developed ways of working in a bounded national vacuum. Instead, and as Elger and Smith also point out, they have continually 'borrowed' from 'Western science and engineering and American management practices' (ibid., p. 32) and vice versa. Sony's distinctiveness is due to the way it attempts to *mix* such elements.

2.2.4   Happy accidents at work: enter the Walkman

So far, much of the material that has been cited in this section might give you the impression that the success of the Walkman was the logical outcome of the inspired activities of a few heroic individuals and due to the peculiarly creative yet controlled culture that had been promulgated within the Sony organization. A somewhat different story, however, is told by Shu Ueyama who was the deputy general manager in Sony's advertising department at the time of the Walkman's introduction.

READING D

You should turn now to the Selected Readings at the end of the book and read 'The selling of the "Walkman"' by Shu Ueyama, an article which first appeared in a trade magazine. When you read this short extract, written by one of the 'participants' in the story, ask yourself a couple of questions about this version of events. Does it sound more convincing than the idea of Akio Morita getting inspiration whilst walking in New York? How 'accidental' was the invention of the Walkman?

Unlike some of our previous discussions about inspired individuals or distinct company cultures, Shu Ueyama explains the appearance of the Walkman as a happy accident that occurred due to a 'routine' organizational change. This change had given the radio–cassette-recorders to the radio division, so staff in the tape-recorder division were 'in trouble'. A new idea was needed in order to revitalize the prestige of the department.

The idea of the Walkman, according to this account, did not come from any moment of inspiration but out of 'serious discussions' that took place 'day and night' and resulted in staff making modifications to existing equipment. In this account you will certainly find the heroic individuals – Masaru Ibuka and Akio Morita are both involved. And you can also read evidence of the company's cultural practice of drawing staff from different divisions and forming them into teams. But, according to Ueyama the *impetus* for the company to come up with the Walkman was a routine organizational change that then led to a rather happy accident.

What did you think when you read the story? We were left with a nagging doubt that the 'accidental' story may be just as partial as the idea of the Walkman coming from the minds of inspired individuals. What we have here is yet another representation of the Walkman story based on luck and accidents. These elements are also *part* of many of the other 'inside' stories that have been re-told about the Walkman (Morita et al., 1987; Kuroki, 1987). If you consult these you will read that the company did not plan the introduction of the Walkman very carefully and that there was a large degree of scepticism about its potential within the company. In his memoirs, Morita recalled that project engineers were reluctant to become involved with the device, that company accountants raised objections to the pricing structure and were worried that the device might not generate sufficient profits to recoup the costs of development. Morita also recalled a general lack of enthusiasm from marketing staff (Morita et al., 1987). Yasuo Kuroki, who was the Director of the Sony Design Centre, also recalled that it 'was not a product we planned or launched carefully' (BBC, 1991).

Despite all this talk of luck and happy accidents, there is much evidence to suggest that considerable financial investment and effort went into the marketing and initial promotion of the Walkman. There may have been some reservations, but a number of sources indicate that there *was* a large amount of careful planning. The representation of the Walkman's appearance as some kind of happy accident in a creative corporate environment needs to be placed alongside the more rational and calculated aspects of the production process.

2.3   Making the Walkman to sell: connecting production and consumption

At this point in our cultural circuit we turn to some of the ways in which 'consumption' is an integral part of the relations of 'production'. Although often separated for the purpose of study and analysis (as in this book), we wish to emphasize the way in which production and consumption are interrelated and overlap. This is an important theoretical issue that has a long history: it is a theme that concerned Karl Marx in his analysis of the relations of capitalist production during the middle of the nineteenth century:

> Production is ... at the same time consumption, and consumption is at the same time production. Each is directly its own counterpart. But at the same time an intermediary movement goes on between the two. Production furthers consumption by creating material for the latter which otherwise would lack its object. But consumption in its turn furthers production, by providing for the products the individual for whom they are products. The product receives its last finishing touches in consumption. A railroad on which no one rides, which is consequently not used up, not consumed, is only a potential railroad ... Without production, no consumption; but, on the other hand, without consumption, no production; since production would then be without a purpose.
>
> (Marx, 1980/1857–8, p. 24)

Following Marx, we could say that a portable stereo that nobody listens to is only a *potential* portable stereo. For it to be fully realized, for it to have any social meaning, production has to be connected to consumption. This is what Stuart Hall, drawing on this particular part of Marx's work, has referred to as 'articulation' – a process of connecting together – in which the dynamic of the 'circuits of production' can be understood as involving an 'articulation of the moments of production, with the moments of consumption, with the moments of realization, with the moments of reproduction' (Hall with Cruz and Lewis, 1994, p. 255). (See also the Introduction to this volume.)

You should bear in mind that whilst we can divide production from consumption for the purpose of study, our analysis should make an attempt to understand how production and consumption are made to 'articulate'. We should attempt to trace the specific dynamics of articulation involved. We will do this here in the following ways. First, by considering how the Walkman was aimed at an imagined consumer who was young. Secondly, by pointing out how the name of the machine was guided by assumptions about consumers' responses to it. Thirdly, we shall consider aspects of marketing and, finally, we shall highlight how Sony attempted to monitor and gain feedback about consumer activity. These will give some indications of what Marx called the 'intermediary movement' that occurs between production and consumption. This will lead into a longer section in which we consider how design is centrally located at this point where production is articulated to consumption.

2.3.1   Assembling for the young consumer: the mothers of the invention

We can start to pursue this issue by considering how the personal stereo-cassette player was initially produced with a specific target audience in mind. A number of accounts of the production of the Walkman indicate that the device was directed at young consumers. It was aimed at those people who already listened to music whilst moving around the home, driving in a car or walking on the street. Observing that young people seemed to need to have music constantly with them, whether in New York or Tokyo, Morita and his colleagues felt that the Walkman would enable people to take their music with them and bring the added advantage that it would not disturb other people.

It was with these considerations in mind that the first Walkmans were produced. A particular *imagined* consumer (based on observation and knowledge of existing patterns of music listening) guided the process of production and also the manufacturing schedule. With a young consumer in mind, the aim was to get the new device into the shops just prior to the school, college and University holidays (Kuroki, 1987). These considerations in turn meant that the small tape-machine had to be marketed at a price that made it affordable for young people.

This consideration about the identity of the envisaged potential consumers of the device thus had a further impact on production: it was important that the price be kept down. The first way in which production was organized to keep costs down was by making all the most important parts (such as motors, stereo-heads and headphones) on site within the company. This eliminated negotiations with suppliers over price and delivery time and enabled the company's management to monitor, oversee and control the processes of production directly (Sony, 1989). Further technical ways were found to reduce costs by using very small integrated circuits instead of individual transistors and resistors. This reduced the number of component parts required and in turn cut both the length of time and the cost of assembling them.

Once the Walkman was in production and selling, there were continual attempts to reduce the cost of production. This culminated in the production of a Walkman Mark 2, launched in February 1981, which was a lighter, smaller model with 50 per cent fewer parts (Borrus, 1987). Technical modifications meant that the time required to assemble the machine was again reduced.

In referring to the process of assembling Walkmans from a number of component parts, we come to a significant contribution to the Walkman's success that is even further removed from the idea of inspired heroes and happy accidents: the routine, rigidly organized and monotonous task carried out by a predominantly female labour force in electronic assembly-plants: see Figure 2.2.

As a number of feminist scholars have argued, the practice of assembling components should not be thought of as simply a secondary activity – as something that just takes place after 'innovation' (Glucksmann, 1990). Instead, assembly-line tasks can be thought of as constituting the 'productive hub' of the manufacturing process. Miriam Glucksmann (1990), for example, points out that ever since the 1920s women assembly-workers have become an increasingly important part of the industrial workforce of the world. Yet the importance and significance of the female assemblers have been undermined by a distinct sexual division of labour in which 'women assemble and men do everything else'. As you will probably have noticed, so far all the 'voices' of the participants in the Sony Walkman story have been male executives. You might recall that some of these men have been referred to as the 'father' of this 'invention'. Here, we might suggest that such fathers are dependent upon the 'mothers' of invention who are found on the assembly-lines.

FIGURE 2.2   On the line: assembling the Sony Walkman.

The production of the Walkman is thus based on a distinctive sexual division of labour. The work of the assembly-line was crucial to the Walkman's initial success. Keeping the costs down depended on controlling the assembly-line and making components that could be assembled rapidly. In this way we can see that the women occupying the assembly-lines have 'a centre-stage significance as workers at the very heart of the production process'

(Glucksmann, 1990, p. 4). Without the women assemblers in their rows in Japan, Malaysia and Taiwan, working away putting components together, the Walkman would not have appeared and would not continue to be manufactured in such large numbers.

2.3.2   Naming the machine: Sony grammar

Earlier we referred to how the company name was chosen to signify a particular identity. The name of the machine was also arrived at as the result of much thought. In his memoirs Morita recalled that he had never liked the name, remarking rather flippantly that he was away on a trip when 'the name was chosen by some young people in our company' (Morita et al., 1987, p. 81). Here again, the eventual name of Walkman did not simply appear in someone's inspired imagination, but was actually derived from existing products, just as the actual technology had been.

Two Sony products in particular were precursors to the Walkman. For some time, Sony had been selling a professional tape-recorder called the 'Pressman'. When the company had initially been developing a prototype of the Walkman, an early version had been produced by stripping the recording circuit and speaker out of the Pressman and replacing it with a stereo amplifier. In addition the phrase 'walkie-talkie' was the name in common usage for the radio-telephones frequently used by the police and medical services. One initial idea for the new, small cassette-machine was to build on this and call it a 'stereo walkie'. However, when company staff started to pursue the patenting of this name they found that Toshiba had already registered the term 'walky' (Kuroki, 1987).

This information caused initial disappointment amongst a number of staff in the company due to the fact that a logo had been created on the theme of walking which featured a pair of walking legs coming out of the bottom of a capital 'A' in the word WALK. This was a very popular design within the company and staff felt that the eventual name should, in some way, enable this design to be retained. Eventually the name Walkman was arrived at and the design with walking legs was

FIGURE 2.3
The walking 'Walkman' logo.

retained but with four legs walking from the 'A's in WALKMAN (see Figure 2.3).

However, some senior staff in the company were concerned about the 'grammar' of the word. Shu Ueyama (1982) has referred to the name Walkman as a 'typical Japanese-made English word'. It is one of those words of 'global English', what Morita had earlier heard as an 'international language' necessary for doing business around the world. As Stuart Hall has written, this is 'English as it has been invaded, and as it has hegemonized a variety of other languages without being able to exclude them from it. It speaks Anglo-Japanese, Anglo-French, Anglo-German … It is a new form of international language' (1991, p. 28).

Despite the development of such a language, Morita remembers that senior Sony personnel in the United States and Britain had serious reservations about the name 'Walkman' and felt that they would not be able to sell a product with such an 'ungrammatical' name. As a result of such judgements, again about an imaginary consumer, the same product was launched with a different name in the United States where it was called the 'Sound-About'. However, the company faced a further problem: Sound-About was already registered in the UK. So, in the United Kingdom the machine was initially promoted as a 'Stowaway'. While it was also launched as Walkman in Asia, the Middle East and Latin America, it was launched as 'Freestyle' in Sweden – staff in Sony Sweden objected to the illicit connotations of the word 'stowaway'.

The use of these different names meant that the same product had to be promoted with separate logos and package designs. In a further effort to cut the costs of production, a decision was made to standardize the name to Walkman throughout the world. However, this was not just an economic decision. Despite their initial doubts, the company had observed that the name was popular and highly memorable and had very quickly started to become a generic term for the small personal cassette-player in much the same way that Hoover had become a term for vacuum-cleaner and Xerox for photocopier.

2.3.3   Marketing and public relations

Earlier we referred to the ways in which advertising is employed in an attempt to encode and fix the meaning of the Walkman in a particular way. Advertising is also employed as part of the repertoire of marketing methods that are used in an attempt to sell the machine; it is used to connect the consumer with the product. However, when the personal stereo was introduced as the Walkman in Japan during July 1979, the company developed a launch strategy that did not involve a large advertising budget. Instead, the company made maximum use of publicity channels. Unlike advertising which is paid for and clearly controlled by the company, publicity is not 'bought' in quite the same way. Public relations work is often harder to identify, yet it can be very effective, particularly when it appears as 'news' or magazine articles (as opposed to advertisements that seem to come directly from the company). In the initial selling of the Walkman, public relations and publicity was far more significant than advertising (Ueyama, 1982). It is here where it becomes clear that the company *did* plan their promotional and marketing activities very carefully. Let us consider some of the specific techniques that were adopted.

First, the company decided that one hundred sets of the new cassette-player should be made available to be distributed free of charge prior to the public launch. These were to be given to potentially influential individuals and considerable thought went into deciding who should receive them. Sets were given to the editors of various magazines, but the company decided to focus attention on musicians, perhaps aware of the significance of Ohga's previous response to the inadequacies of the reel-to-reel tape-recorder. It was also thought that touring musicians were a particularly important target group as they listened to music on their travels; in order to do this, musicians would often resort to carrying rather cumbersome tape-machines with them when travelling. Sets were therefore given away to leading musicians in Japan and also to visiting musicians from overseas. In particular, Walkman sets were given to members of the Berlin Philharmonic and New York Philharmonic Orchestras who, so the story goes, were impressed and took the sets back to their countries to spread the news further by word of mouth. Prior to its launch in the United States, knowledge of the Walkman was also taken to the US by tourists returning with sets that they had purchased on visits to Japan (Dreyfack, 1981).

Listening was also emphasized when the press were invited to the launch of the Walkman. The invitations were sent out on audiocassettes, rather than the usual invitation card or press release, and members of the press and broadcast media were invited to attend Sony's corporate headquarters. From this location a sightseeing bus took the assembled journalists to Yoyogi Park where they were set down to watch teenagers wearing Walkmans whilst roller-skating. In addition to this visit to the park, the company had also arranged for the journalists to listen to the Walkman in specially produced cubicles.

A further promotional tactic involved the company paying couples to stroll through Tokyo's busy, largely pedestrianized Ginza shopping district whilst listening to their Walkmans (Morita et al., 1987, p. 81). The company, in collaboration with broadcasters, also conducted various *vox pop* interviews with visitors to Japan who were approached and encouraged to proffer their responses to the new cassette-player. Their reactions were duly video-taped and featured in news broadcasts.

Through these publicity-producing exercises, Sony staff sought to present the Walkman in a very specific way. The machine was presented with meanings that were attractive both to journalists wanting an interesting angle for a news story, and to the target group of mobile, young music-listeners. Having put such ideas in circulation with the Walkman's launch, Sony also attempted to monitor responses to the machine.

2.3.4 Monitoring consumption and market research

A further way in which 'production' and 'consumption' are brought together and connected is through market research and a variety of feedback monitoring systems. On this point, the company carried out more systematic research than has sometimes been implied. Over the years, Akio Morita made a habit of telling journalists that Sony did not conduct market research. When writing of the Walkman in his memoirs, he commented:

> The public does not know what is possible, but we do. So instead of doing a lot of market research, we refine our thinking on a product and its use and try to create a market for it by educating and communicating with the public ... I do not believe that any amount of market research could have told us that the Sony Walkman would be successful.

> (Morita et al., 1987, pp. 79–82)

Somewhat in contrast to this, in his own memoirs Yasuo Kuroki (1987) reports that, whilst Sony had tended not to conduct market research in the past, the company *did* decide to do research on the Walkman. This was done by recruiting young people and giving them the small tape-machine and instructing them on how to use it. The researchers would then simply allow the young person to use the machine and observe what ensued. From a total of one hundred people who were researched in this way, Kuroki remembers that one in every five immediately started moving rhythmically to the music and that a large number of these users expressed surprise at the quality of the sound. This aspect was actively promoted by the company in their television advertising campaigns which stressed people's disbelief at the sound quality of such a small cassette-player (Kuroki, 1987).

Once the machine was selling, however, it was retailers and Sony dealers who started providing some of the first feedback to the company on how Walkmans were being used and who was purchasing them. There are two issues here that show how production and consumption interact and how this can lead to changes to the actual product. First, a wider range of people were using the devices than Sony's imagined young consumer. Second, the device was being used in a more individualistic way than the company initially anticipated.

During 1981 the trade publication *Merchandising* reported that personal stereos were selling faster than had been expected and reviewed some of the comments of retailers about who was purchasing Walkmans. Typical was the retailer who observed: 'We have customers ranging from 18 to 60. Some are bikers, roller skaters, skateboarders, hikers or just out for a walk. We're only seven miles from the beach and because of the warm weather all kinds of people are outdoors and want to listen to music' (Stearns, 1981, p. 91). Another retailer reported that they were selling to 'all kinds of people', but particularly to those engaging in outdoor activities such as riding bikes, skiing and jogging (Blood, 1981, p. 93). Sony immediately took account of such feedback and began to incorporate the image of outdoor activity in the country, for example, into their advertising, recognizing the Walkman's potential appeal for an identity that had not been part of the initial imagined consumer.

One of the most conspicuous ways that consumption fed back into production was due to the way that the Walkman was used in a more 'personal', individualistic and less interactive way than was initially imagined. Partly on the advice of Akio Morita, the first version of the Walkman had contained two headphone jack sockets so that two people could listen to the same machine simultaneously. Morita's reasoning was driven by his belief that it would be considered rude or discourteous for one person to listen to music alone. This conception of the imagined consumer was represented in the some of the first press advertisements for the Walkman and the Stowaway.

In the first Japanese television campaign, a commercial was produced that depicted a 'very tall American woman and an old Japanese gentleman' who were both wearing headphones connected to the same Walkman from which they were sharing the music (Ueyama, 1982). (See Figure 1.1 and the discussion of this advertisement in section 1.) Not long afterwards, the press advertisements for the Stowaway informed readers that the new stereo cassette-players had been designed with facilities for two sets of headphones 'which means that you and a friend can listen at the same time ... The TPS-L2 [first model] even features a hotline, enabling you to talk to your partner without removing the headphones or lowering the volume'. The accompanying advertising included photographs of a man and woman riding a tandem (each wearing Walkmans) and a loving couple staring into each others' eyes (whilst wearing Walkmans) in front of a sea/sunset scene. It was only after the Walkman was launched and being used that Morita observed that 'buyers began to see their little portable stereo sets as very personal' (Morita et al., 1987, p. 81). As a result, the Walkman Mk2 was introduced as a machine with just one headphone jack socket.

The Walkman, then, was not simply presented as a device for individual listening – it *became* this through a process in which production and consumption were articulated. The technology was not simply produced as a finished artefact which then had an impact on consumption. Consumer activities were crucial to the introduction, modification and subsequent redevelopment and marketing of this product. As we have stressed in this section, the processes of production only provide a series of possibilities that have to be realized in and through consumption. In the process, the company constantly seeks to take account of and respond to the ways in which consumers are 'appropriating' the products. Part of the Walkman's success was down to the way in which Sony responded to the uses of the Walkman and integrated this knowledge 'into' production. In so doing, they brought together two parts of the cultural circuit that are often thought of as separate. As production and consumption articulated, the product received its 'finishing touches'. In turn, it was re-designed as a result of the ways in which it was being used in consumption. Hence, designers occupy a place as important' cultural intermediaries at the interface between production and consumption.

DESIGNING THE WALKMAN: ARTICULATING PRODUCTION AND CONSUMPTION

3.1   Designers as cultural intermediaries

So far we have outlined some of the accounts which can be found of the origins of the Walkman and we have explained how its origins – quite typically for a successful technology – are bound up in numerous, often contradictory, narratives. In discussing the design of the Walkman, our interest is not with *who* designed it, but with what its design embodies or represents – in other words, with how its very design 'makes meaning'.

Our first task is to clarify what a designer is. One of the most common assumptions is that the designer is some sort of artist. Nearly all the literature on design is concerned with aesthetics; it uses much the same language as is used in discussing art. But designers are different from artists because their main purpose is to make artefacts attractive so that they sell. To make artefacts sell, as we shall see in the case of the Walkman, designers have to *embody* culture in the things they design. Designed artefacts are certainly there to *do* something, they are often functional (for playing tapes, for instance); but, more than this, they are inscribed with *meanings* as well as uses. So, in addition to creating artefacts with a specific function, designers are also in the game of making those artefacts meaningful. In other words, design produces meaning through encoding artefacts with symbolic significance; it gives functional artefacts a symbolic form. Designers are key **cultural intermediaries**, to use the terminology of the cultural theorist Pierre Bourdieu (1984).

cultural intermediaries

By the term 'cultural intermediaries' Bourdieu is referring to that increasingly important group of workers who play an active role in promoting consumption through attaching to products and services particular meanings and 'lifestyles' with which consumers will identify. Put simply, they can be defined as people involved in the provision of *symbolic* goods and services. They are most frequently found in the media, fashion, advertising and design industries. In their symbolic work of making products 'meaningful', designers are a key link in our cultural circuit; for, amongst many other things, they articulate production and the world of engineers with the market and consumers. Indeed, the perpetual attempt to achieve that magic 'fit' between production and consumption is often represented as the 'holy grail' of the designer (Gardner and Sheppard, 1989, p. 74).

3.2   The organization of design at Sony

Sony is an organization which is both represented and represents itself as the paradigm of a 'design-led' corporation (Morita et al., 1987; Sparke, 1987; Aldersey-Williams, 1992). Design at Sony, it is often claimed, is *organized* in a way which enables the company to make products which both create and respond to consumer 'needs' in a highly flexible manner. There are three elements of the organization of design at Sony which have been represented as providing the key to its success in achieving this 'fit' between production and consumption.

First, the functional and occupational status of design and designers at Sony is held to be greater – particularly vis-à-vis that of engineering and engineers – than at other comparable organizations. Until comparatively recently the status of design within the occupational hierarchy of many manufacturing corporations was considerably lower than that of engineers, the influence of the former being confined to styling and a little ergonomics. Secondly, designers at Sony have enjoyed relatively easy access to senior management and, indeed, have become the most senior of managers – again, most unusual in a manufacturing organization. Thirdly, design at Sony has been organized in such a way that designers are kept closely in touch with contemporary cultural trends and with the cultural practices of target consumer groupings.

We can begin to gauge the importance of these first two elements by focusing upon the design 'hub' at Sony: the Design or PP – Product Planning, Product Proposal and Product Presentation – Centre. The multiple meanings contained within the acronym 'PP' suggest the extended role that design plays within the Sony corporation. Product design at Sony involves production and marketing within its remit – in other words, it is involved in developing entire product concepts – as well as the usual styling function, thus guaranteeing it a more strategic role than that usually attributed to design within manufacturing organizations. It is possible to understand the centrality of design at Sony when we turn our attention to the role that the Design Centre played in the creation of the most popular of the Sony Walkman range, the 'classic' Walkman II (WM-2).

When the term Sony Walkman is mentioned, it is rarely the original Walkman that people recall – the TPS-L2 (see Figure 3.1); rather it is the WM-2 (see Figure 3.2). Its design, which deviated quite distinctly from that typical of cassette-players, is deemed by Sony, amongst others, to have firmly 'established the new product concept of the Walkman' (Sony, 1989).

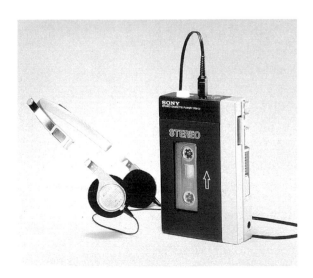

FIGURE 3.1 The original Walkman, the TPS-L2.

FIGURE 3.2 The 'classic' Walkman II, the WM-2.

The design, which features switches located at the front of the machine rather than at the side, was developed by the Sony Design Centre as an entry for a commercial design competition. This model also had another original feature: the tapehead was installed on the back of the cassette housing cover. This mechanism, which assured that the tape made even contact with the head when inserted, achieved considerable space-savings over the conventional mechanism in the TPS-L2 which moved the head when the playback button was pushed down. Although the model had originally been envisaged as a cassette tape-recorder, the company decided to use the design for the next generation of Sony Walkmans.

Conventionally, as we have already indicated, product development begins with the general locational requirements of basic mechanisms and switches specified by engineers, and then the designers incorporate them into their design development. At Sony, because of the centrality of the Design Centre within the overall organizational structure, the design development of the WM-2 was turned upside down, with the engineers required to work within the parameters specified in advance by the Design Centre – including body size and layout of switches.

As a result, the body of the WM-2 weighed only 280 grams (9.9 oz). This made it 110 grams (3.9 oz) lighter than the original TPS-L2 model and very close to the conceptual image of the size of two 'AA' batteries and an audiocassette that is represented in so much of Sony's advertising and publicity material for the Walkman (remember Figure 1.3 where the Walkman is represented as 'a cassette player so small you could hide it behind a cassette box'?). Brought onto the market in 1982, the WM-2 has since achieved sales of over 2.5 million units and remains the best-selling Walkman model of all time.

The role of the Design Centre in creating the WM-2 indicates the important position that design occupies within Sony. Rather than simply developing the ideas and specifications of engineers and others, the Design Centre was the initiator of the entire product concept. According to the former head of design at Sony, Yasuo Kuroki, the Design Centre was not limited to look and shape. The whole concept – how a product is sold, how a product is marketed, how a product is advertised – really developed there. In this way, design at Sony does not just 'add value' to existing technology, but has been a fundamental element of product innovation, linking the complex worlds of production and consumption.

Not only has the design function occupied a central position within the overall organizational structure of Sony, individual designers have also played crucial roles in the management of the organization. Yasuo Kuroki, for example, head of the Design Centre during the early days of the Walkman's development and production, was the only departmental head at Sony who reported directly to Akio Morita's deputy, Norio Ohga. And Ohga, himself a former head of design at Sony, later became President of the corporation.

As we indicated earlier, design at Sony is also organized to stay close to the cultural practices and preferences of target consumer groupings, focusing designers on reading the 'signs on the street' as well as concentrating on the function and form of product concepts. As Kuroki's comments above indicate, design at Sony is not simply concerned with creating functionally apposite and intelligible products but with specifiying design that symbolizes subjects and meanings beyond the ones that are obvious. As one commentator has argued, seen in this way the designer is a 'radar – scanning art, architecture, technology, fashion, pop, everything and … translating it into design' (Powell quoted in Gardner and Sheppard, 1989, p. 74).

At Sony there are a number of ways in which this scanning takes place. We have already mentioned the importance of market research in the targeting of the Walkman (see section 2.3.4). Another way, and one in which designers are heavily implicated, is through the Sony Showroom concept. Located in some of the world's 'global cities' – Tokyo, New York and Paris, for example – Sony's showrooms are part shop, part playground and part R&D laboratory. In a highly 'designed' environment – furnished with 'lifestyle settings' such as bedrooms, offices, lounges – consumers are encouraged to walk in and play with Sony products, to be assisted in using them if they so desire and, at the same time, their behaviour and preferences are monitored by Sony staff.

In the Chicago showroom, for example, staff meet daily to discuss consumer reactions to different products. The information is then passed on to Sony headquarters where it can be used to refine the design of products yet to go to market or to develop new marketing and merchandising strategies for existing products (Miller, 1992, p. 2). Through encouraging consumers to interact with products in a space that does not have the threatening appearance of a shop – in other words, where people will not feel an overt pressure to purchase – Sony hopes to see consumers using technology as they would in their everyday lives. This is important to Sony because the more 'realistic' the reaction in this environment – whether good or bad – the more likely it is that this reaction might be enhanced or modified with suitable adjustments in design, or in marketing and so on. In this sense, the showroom is very much a laboratory designed to further articulate production with consumption.

3.3   Lifestyling the Walkman

As we saw in our discussion of advertising, in section 1.8, and of marketing, in section 2.3.4, these forms of symbolic expertise attempt to sell products through addressing consumers as certain sorts of subjects. The language of advertising and marketing attempts to create *identification* between consumer and product. It inscribes or encodes the product with meanings with which it is hoped consumers will identify. Design operates in a similar way. The visual 'look' and tactile 'feel' of a product are crucial means of communicating with consumers, not simply about function or basic 'use' but simultaneously about identity and meaning. Design in a very fundamental way speaks on behalf of the product to the consumer. It addresses the consumer as a certain sort of person.

We can better understand how design works to encode a product with a particular meaning or identity by focusing upon the massive expansion in the range of Sony Walkmans available for consumption since the launch of the original model in 1979. In particular, we will focus upon the role of design in 'lifestyling' a range of Sony products – including two versions of the Walkman – targeted at young children, what the company terms their 'My First Sony' range.

As we indicated in sections 1 and 2, the Walkman was originally designed for and marketed to a particular target consumer grouping: mobile, young music-listeners. However, as we saw in section 2.3.4, the company soon became aware that a much more diverse range of people than had originally been envisaged were actually purchasing and using the Walkman. As Sony began to realize that there was more than one market for the Walkman, its advertising strategy, for example, underwent a subtle change of emphasis – appealing to lovers of outdoor pursuits in the country and not simply to urban youth. Sony recognized, in effect, that the Walkman had an appeal for an identity beyond that of the initial imagined consumer.

Gradually, as Walkman sales increased worldwide it was not simply *representations* of the Walkman that began to change but the *very 'look' and 'feel' of the product itself*. In other words, Sony shifted from registering the increasing diversity of consumer use through changes in its advertising and marketing materials alone to inscribing those changes onto the 'body' of the Walkman itself, through changes in its *design*. Instead of a single Walkman model sold worldwide, Sony began to customize the product, targeting different sorts of Walkman at different consumer markets. Or to put it another way, Sony began to **lifestyle** the Walkman.

lifestyle

So what does the term 'lifestyle' mean in this context? Well, basically, the term refers to the combination of responsive design and visual communication with techniques of market segmentation. In contrast with selling the same basic model to a mass market, lifestyling involves tailoring or customizing a product to the lifestyle of a particular niche or target market segment. Lifestyling is also made possible by the development of new methods of production linked to novel forms of flexible, electronics-based automation technologies, often referred to as 'flexible specialization' (Piore and Sabel, 1984). In contrast to mass production techniques, where particular products were manufactured in large batches on assembly-lines that required great investment in inflexible plant, flexible specialization techniques make small batch production possible. So whereas in the past motor companies, for example, would produce one model of a particular car, nowadays using computer-based technologies and a functionally flexible labour force, it is common for a particular model to be available in a large number of different versions, each designed for and marketed at a distinct consumer grouping.

We can see this combination of new production technologies, responsive design and market segmentation operating at Sony where the Walkman is now available in over seven hundred versions. There are Walkmans for all tastes and prices: they can be solar-powered, waterproof, and attachable to a sweatband (for racquet sports); they come designed specifically for skiing, jogging or camping; they can come with a clock and/or a radio; they are even available in gold! (See Figure 3.3.)

One of the most publicized of Sony's 'lifestyling' initiatives was its decision in 1987 to create a range of products aimed specifically at young children – the 'My First Sony' range. Taking a closer look at this initiative can help us to understand better how designers encode products with particular meanings and more generally how the practice of 'lifestyling' works.

> READING E
>
> You should turn now to the article entitled 'How Sony Corp. became first with kids' which is reproduced in the Selected Readings at the end of the book.

In this article a senior executive at Sony describes how the company set about developing a line of products aimed specifically at children. One of their primary objectives in targeting this group appears to have been the desire to build 'brand loyalty' from a young age. By getting children – through their parents – to identify with Sony products from their earliest years, the company hoped to keep those consumers on board for the rest of their lives. The very title of the range – 'My First Sony' – connotes a potential life-long relationship between company and consumer. From cradle to grave, it seems to be suggesting, Sony will have a product for you at every stage of your life.

Although the products were designed for use by young children, the company defined its target audience as being 'adults, generally working couples who are reasonably affluent'. As young children generally have their consumption mediated by their parents, Sony aimed their marketing and advertising materials mainly at parents – and middle-class parents specifically – advertising on television at times when both parents would be assumed to be viewing, rather than children alone, and deliberately placing cute 'embraceable' kids in the frame who were thought likely to elicit a favourable emotional response, especially from women.

The company was also keen to stress that the 'My First Sony' range did not represent a move by Sony into the toy business. Rather, they stressed that the range was a 'niche' within their wider market of 'quality' consumer electronics. This stress on 'quality' can be found in the advertising materials used to promote the range. One campaign in Australia appealed directly to parents in the name of quality, establishing a chain of meaning between the quality of Sony's products, high-quality parenting and a child's quality of life. Your children, the copy boldly pronounced, are 'Never too young to experience the best'.

FIGURE 3.3
The many faces of the Walkman.

The Solar Walkman (F-107) with TV/FM/AM (shown in three colours – yellow, white and pale blue). In the US, where there are over 4000 FM radio stations, about 80 per cent of Walkmans sold include this function.

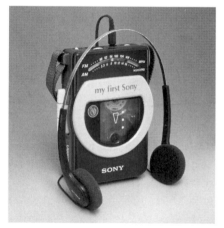

The 'My First Sony'™ concept developed in the US and targeted at children. Several models of Walkman belong to this line, produced in the primary colours of red, yellow and blue.

The bright yellow waterproof Sports Walkman(WMF-F5) is extremely popular on the US West Coast, Canada and Sweden.

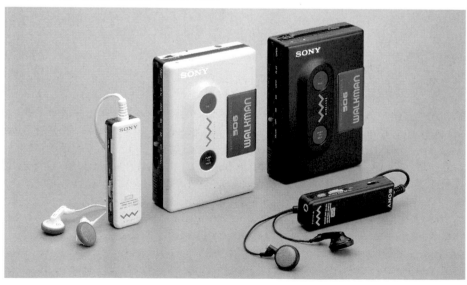

Introduced in Japan, this wireless type (WM-500) invented by Sony is gaining popularity.

Reading E also highlights the important role that cultural intermediaries played in developing the product range. From the focus groups which marketeers ran to assess parents' views about the desirability and market potential of the range, through to the advertising strategy aimed at appealing to middle-class parents as typical purchasers of the products, symbolic expertise played a crucial role in creating the market for 'My First Sony'. For our purposes, it is the role of design in this 'lifestyling' process that is of most interest.

As we can see, design operated on the very cusp of production and consumption, attempting to stitch the two spheres together. On the one hand, designers were charged with translating adult models of basic Sony products – such as the Walkman – into products suitable for children. This involved considerable work not simply of a 'technical' kind, utilizing more durable materials and making 'sharp' edges more rounded and hence less likely to cause injury, but also of a cultural kind – constructing a 'look' for the products – in this case using bright primary colours – that would appeal to children of both sexes. On the other hand, the design team did not just work within the sphere of production – creating products in their offices – they also spent time in retail toy-stores observing, for example, the behaviour of parents and children at first hand. This first-hand observation not only contributed to their decisions concerning the look of the actual products, but also to their choice of packaging and visual presentation.

Overall, through their deployment of a range of competencies – technical and cultural and operating in the domains of both production and consumption – designers played a crucial role in translating a number of fairly disparate adult electronic products into a niche range of children's goods, with their own distinct 'brand identity'. Or, to put it another way, through the deployment of their particular 'symbolic' expertise, designers made a series of products achieve a new **register of meaning.**

register of meaning

3.4   The Walkman: how 'Japanese' is it?

So far we have been discussing the work of designers as cultural intermediaries generally and their role within the Sony Corporation and in the creation of the Walkman in particular. As we saw in section 3.2, Sony is a company that has been represented – and represents itself – as a design-led corporation. It is often claimed that only a Japanese company like Sony, where design is allocated such a central position within the organizational structure and culture, could have created a material cultural artefact like the Walkman (Morita et al., 1987; BBC, 1991). However, this is only one strand of an argument concerning the presumed 'Japaneseness' of the Walkman. This particular argument is often supplemented by another which suggests that the Walkman embodies in its design certain national cultural characteristics that are peculiarly 'Japanese'. In other words, it is argued not simply that the Walkman could only have emerged from a Japanese organization (you may remember that we discussed the merits of this particular argument in section 2.2.3 above), but that it could only have emerged from Japan because certain 'cultural' characteristics it embodies – its minute size, for example – are inherently 'Japanese'.

In this section we will explore this argument to see to what extent it is reasonable to describe the design of Walkman as essentially 'Japanese'. We can begin this task by examining some of the design traits that are often represented as distinctively Japanese and which the Walkman in particular is said to embody. We will focus on two such design characteristics: miniaturization and an aesthetic of simplicity and attention to detail.

Compactness, simplicity and fine detailing have been consistently represented as central features of Japanese design (see Figure 3.4). Rooted in particular practices and expressed in particular material cultural artefacts – in the rituals of the tea ceremony, in the cultivation of the Bonsai, or in the spiritual exercises of Zen Buddhism, for example – they are held to provide a frame of reference or a tradition which has given Japanese culture a distinctive coherence and shape over time and which has helped to mark it off from other, different, but similarly well-bounded cultures (BBC, 1991; Tobin, 1992).

As we mentioned above, the Walkman has often been represented as the latter-day embodiment of this 'traditional' Japanese design aesthetic. Its small size and the simplicity of its visual 'look' are invoked as typically 'Japanese' attributes (Morita et al., 1987; BBC, 1991). In these accounts, the Walkman design is seen to express certain core elements or 'essences' of Japanese cultural identity that have stayed exactly the same over time. According to the former head of the Sony Design Centre, Yasuo Kuroki, for example, the early Walkman model clearly drew upon Japanese tradition in that it used simple

Figure 3.4
Traditional Japanese tableware.

colours (especially black) and had a linear form – reflecting traditional tatami mats with their straight lines (BBC, 1991).

This notion of 'tradition' as a sort of umbilical cord stretching from the present – in the shape of the Walkman and other 'modern' products – to some point of origin in the dim, distant past has been consistently deployed by western commentators eager to explain the 'Japanese economic miracle'. As Morley and Robins (1992) have indicated, in contrast to certain presumed characteristics of western societies – a liberal culture of individualism and pluralism, for example – Japan is frequently represented in the western media and in popular cultural texts as a culture of conformity, of ethnic purity, and of homogeneity, with the Japanese portrayed as an austere, highly disciplined, almost robotic people. 'They' are different from 'us', it is argued, because they are still very 'traditional'. This is the source of 'their' success and 'our' danger. At the same time a similar discourse of 'tradition' has also been utilized quite strategically by Japanese commentators – including members of Sony's senior management and design teams – to create and sustain a sense of corporate and national identity through signifying Japan's difference from the 'West' (Morita et al., 1987).

However, this closed and homogeneous notion of tradition may not be as unambiguous and unidimensional as it seems. Looked at more closely, 'Japanese design' shows clear signs of being a much more complex and culturally hybrid category than it might at first appear. Rather than being a water-tight 'tradition' clearly bounded off from other cultures, the category of 'Japanese design' has historically been constituted through extensive contact with the West, most notably as a result of invasion and occupation.

Post-war Japanese industrial design, for example, was crucially influenced by the American occupation. As a number of commentators have argued, the development of Japanese manufacturing after the Second World War was shaped by the presence of the US, and industrial design was no exception (Barnet and Cavanagh, 1994). Indeed, no lesser a body than the Japanese Industrial Design Association (1983) has indicated that to a considerable extent 'industrial design was ... embedded in the minds of the Japanese by the occupying forces of America'.

As far as 'Japanese design' is concerned, the post-war period of reconstruction was a time of considerable dislocation and discontinuity with priorities being set within a framework dictated largely by the US. It is significant that the corporations, such as Sony, that grew up during this period – and that are now recognized as Japan's design leaders – did not embody Japanese 'tradition' in designing their products. Rather, designs during this period were largely derived from existing western styles. For example, the first transistor radio created by Sony (the TR-55) utilized US styling (see Figures 3.5 and 3.6); similarly, the first Japanese produced cameras were careful copies of the German 35mm Leica (Aldersey-Williams, 1992).

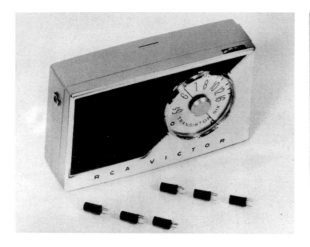
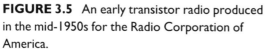

FIGURE 3.5 An early transistor radio produced in the mid-1950s for the Radio Corporation of America.

FIGURE 3.6 The TR-55 transistor radio, Sony's first export, owed much to US styling.

To the extent that contemporary Japanese industrial design is framed by that post-war experience, it cannot be described simply as 'traditional', for it has been constituted in relation to the dominance of western and particularly American and German conceptions of what industrial design is and should be. In other words, Japanese design is not a tradition that has stayed the same throughout time, but rather it is a transculturated phenomenon. By **transculturation** we refer to a term borrowed from ethnographers to describe 'how subordinated … groups select and invent from materials transmitted to them by a dominant or metropolitan culture' (Pratt, 1992, p. 7). As with the cross-breeding of a plant from different strains, this process of transculturation is sometimes referred to as **hybridization**.

transculturation

hybridization

So what about the Walkman? To what extent is that product Japanese? As we have already indicated, the two characteristic features of the Walkman most frequently referred to as expressing traditional 'Japaneseness' are its size and its aesthetic of simplicity and attention to detail. However, the idea that these elements of Walkman design make it unambiguously 'Japanese' has been challenged from a number of quarters, most powerfully by Japanese designers themselves. According to industrial designer Kozo Sato, for example, these characteristic features of products such as the Walkman are less the embodiment of some innate Japanese craft ideal and more the product of diligent market research and a design education centred on western aesthetic values (Sato in Aldersey-Williams, 1992, p. 148).

Sato suggests that contemporary Japanese industrial design successes can be traced to the country's government-fostered post-war efforts to build up export markets and to use design as a weapon in the armoury of Japanese competitiveness. He credits Japanese design successes such as the Walkman more to post-war borrowings and translations from the West, in particular US and German designs, than to any inherent 'traditionalism'. This is not to deny the existence of a distinct design aesthetic at Sony and other Japanese corporations or of a distinct set of Japanese aesthetic traditions, but it is to suggest that that aesthetic is not 'traditionally' Japanese, *in the sense of being a closed, bounded cultural practice impervious to 'foreign' influences.* Instead it should be seen as a hybrid product of transculturation. Compared with the watertight way in which the category 'Japanese' is commonly contrasted with the 'West', the reality is of extensive import and export in the creation of Japanese (as any other) design culture.

Rather than being the product of a closed, homogeneous, national tradition, then, the Walkman is perhaps better viewed as a global material cultural artefact. As Sato's comments above suggest, Japanese design is not a 'pure' category; it has no timeless 'essence'. Japanese designers have drawn and continue to draw upon a variety of cultural influences from around the world in creating 'Japanese' products for an increasingly global market place.

In contrast to Yasuo Kuroki's comments about the essential link between the Walkman and traditional Japanese design, another Walkman designer, Masayoshi Tsuchiya, tells a different, somewhat more 'transculturated', story (quoted in Aldersey-Williams, 1992). Tsuchiya played a crucial role in the design of the Walkman WM-109. While he admits that the double-painted metal of the final product tries to capture the brittle blue whiteness of a 'traditional' Japanese ceramic chopstick holder, he does not interpret his use of this object as expressing his or the Walkman's essential Japaneseness. Instead, the link with 'tradition' is much more ambiguous.

FIGURE 3.7
The Walkman
WM-109.

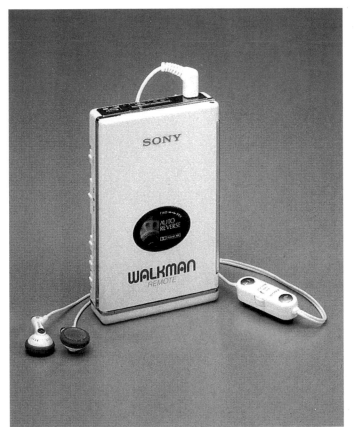

Tsuchiya says the idea for the WM-109 design was initially derived from a striking fashion photo. Although this photo formed the basis for the design, it was the 'look' of the chopstick holder that provided him with the 'suitable finish' he wanted for the product. Thus, his relationship to the 'traditional' ceramic was not an 'essential' one but rather more contingent. He remarks that he was 'casting around' for a suitable finish and just happened to be 'struck by the appearance of a ceramic chopstick holder'. Rather than consciously and deliberately reproducing 'tradition', Tsuchiya appears to have come upon the idea of using the chopstick holder as part of a somewhat more eclectic and 'international' design practice – that practice we noted earlier of 'scanning' a diversity of sources and combining elements from them in the design of a particular product. In this sense the WM-109 is very much a hybrid creation.

As the link between territory and culture becomes more tenuous, design becomes an increasingly 'global' language, with practitioners in any given 'nation' drawing upon a range of signifiers from all over the world in their work. In this environment, pure, unified, watertight national 'design traditions' are increasingly difficult to envisage. This does not mean that the category 'Japanese design' is a misnomer. It simply means that that category needs to be thought about and represented differently, i.e. non-traditionally. If we think about the Walkman, for example, we cannot deny that it has become associated with 'Japan'. However, we can say that this might be due less to the ways in which it *reflects* the timeless essence of some Japanese tradition than it is to the ways in which Japanese designers create products that come to be represented as typically 'Japanese'. It is through such products as the Walkman that miniaturization comes to be associated with Japan rather than through minitiaturizaton that a Japanese essence is inscribed onto the Walkman.

SONY AS A GLOBAL FIRM

4.1   Following the Walkman: competition and financial crisis

Having considered the production and design of the Walkman in some detail, we now seek to emphasize the importance of locating these processes in a wider context. Conceptually, we are concerned in this section with the way in which Sony as an organization, and hence the ongoing production of the Walkman after its initial phase of production and design, is located within a wider set of cultural relationships. To do this, we shall use the concepts of globalization and the culture industry. We start with a situation that you may not have anticipated from what you have read so far, or from your own perception of the success of the Sony Walkman: having launched a successful consumer technology which began selling faster than expected, you might expect that Sony would have enjoyed immediate financial success. However, after the introduction of the Walkman in 1979, quite the opposite happened: Sony experienced a financial crisis – profits dropped repeatedly each year from 1980 to 1983.

In part, the company's problems were due to the broader slump in the world economy which occurred at the beginning of the 1980s. But the company was also affected by increasing competition and, as a result, was over-burdened with the cost of heavy investment in research and development which were not being offset by profits. The personal stereo was not the only new product that Sony had invested resources in developing, manufacturing and launching during this period. The company had also developed the Betamax videocassette-recorder. This machine was generally considered to be technically superior to the alternative VHS system that had been developed and introduced by Sony's Japanese rival, Matsushita. However, Sony increasingly lost their share of the market to Matsushita's VHS format due to the way in which a number of Sony's competitors supported the alternative format and, crucially, due to the fact that companies chose to release films on one system – VHS – rather than in both formats.

Sony had also developed the Trinitron colour television during this period, but not long after its launch numerous competing versions from a range of other companies also came onto the market. In addition, Sony had spent an estimated $25 million developing the compact disc and player, a project completed in collaboration with Philips. Again, this began to be produced by a number of other manufacturers within a very short period after its launch.

Sony were thus investing heavily in the research and development of new products. In the past, it had been usual for the company to recoup this expenditure during the early years of a new product's life. At the beginning, when there was little competition, a new product could be priced highly – at a 'premium' price for a new and exclusive product. However, by the beginning of the 1980s Sony was facing increasing competition in the consumer electronics market, particularly from other Japanese and Pacific Rim companies. This meant that prices were being forced down much earlier in a product's sales life. Sony was consequently finding it more difficult to recoup the initial investment in research and development. In contrast, its competitors – who had not invested in developing the technology in the first place – were able to manufacture their own versions without needing to recoup large accumulated overheads from research and development.

When Sony introduced the Walkman, it *did* take their competitors some time to come up with their own versions. But within two years fifty competitors had put their own machines on to the market (Dreyfack, 1981). From this moment on the competition accelerated dramatically. As *Forbes* magazine observed in 1983, 'Sony could once count on two or three years' technological monopoly to reap the reward of its brilliant inventions. Now competitors catch up in four to eight months' (Cieply, 1983, p. 130).

These pressures led to an internal and external reorganization of Sony's operations, as an attempt to make the company more profitable. The changes that were introduced after the Walkman was launched provide an indication of two important dimensions to the business environment in which the Walkman had appeared. The first of these goes by the name of 'globalization'. The second, involves the concept of hardware–software 'synergy'. We will briefly refer to each of these terms in turn and indicate how they tell us something more about the cultural life of the Sony Walkman.

4.2   Sony goes global and local

We have already seen how Sony initially launched the Walkman locally in Japan, and followed this by introducing it under different brand names into other countries. When Sony standardized the name to Walkman in the early 1980s this occurred at a moment when a number of major companies were beginning to standardize the names of products that had previously been marketed with different labels around the world (this has sometimes been spoken of as 'global' branding and 'global' advertising). However, Sony did not standardize just the *name* of their product, they also introduced two other significant policies at the same time, which were part of a more 'global' approach to the product and the company's operations more generally.

First, the company introduced an international warranty system which meant that Sony products, no matter where they had been purchased, could be repaired or replaced by Sony service agents in other countries. Second, they standardized the cassette-player's electronics so that it would run on two dry-cell batteries. This meant that different models would not be dependent upon the different electricity systems operating in different parts of the world. As ex-advertising executive Shu Ueyama (1982) recalled, 'These factors encouraged the casual purchasing of the Walkman from a discount shop in Tokyo or in New York or at an airport shop in Hong Kong.'

This 'globalizing' strategy was part of a more general approach which the company had been pursuing since Morita and Ibuka started travelling backwards and forwards between Japan and the United States during the 1950s. Sony were attempting at the same time to standardize – produce the same packaging and advertise a universal 'global' brand – and to individualize – by responding to the different ways in which products were being used around the world by designing a range of models of the Walkman for different markets and lifestyles.

Sony were pursuing such aims at a moment when the term **globalization** was gaining increasing currency amongst business commentators and corporate strategists and, like a number of other companies, Sony began to incorporate such discourses into their own company literature. Senior executives began referring to Sony as a 'global' company. Morita continually gave interviews in which he spoke of globalization, once explaining, 'I use the term because I don't like the word multinational … If it means a company with many nationalities then that is not Sony. Sony is global' (Cope, 1990, p. 53). Such a comment led to the suggestion that Morita's talk of globalization was less about any significant organizational change, but more an attempt to shift away from the negative connotations that the term 'multinational corporation' had started to assume.

globalization

The term 'globalization' has acquired a variety of meanings within and across a number of different discourses. Although initially adopted as a buzzword for a business strategy during the 1970s, the label has come to be used more generally in intellectual debate to refer to both a *process* and a *condition*. The process of globalization refers to the way in which media texts (sounds, images, words), capital, technologies, individuals and social groups seem to be moving across the world more rapidly and in greater numbers than in the past. The *condition* of globalization is generally used by writers who argue that human activities are converging and being shared to the extent that the planet is becoming 'one world' (Giddens, 1990, p. 77).

However, no one person or perspective can fully know 'the world' and no company can ever actually *be* global in anything but a partial way. Any case-study that seeks to employ the concept of globalization therefore needs to approach the issue carefully in terms of the particular 'global' processes that are relevant to the case.

In this specific study we have already referred to a number of 'global' dynamics within which the Walkman was produced, marketed and interpreted. We have highlighted how the growth of Sony as a company and its technologies occurred within a process of interaction between the United States and Japan. Akio Morita and his colleagues grew up in a world in which US products and cultural forms were ever present, and in which the development of manufacturing industry in Japan was restricted and monitored by the United States. As the company grew, Sony executives gained considerable knowledge from constant visits to the US, acquired the rights to produce the transistor from the US and found that North America provided a major market for their audio-visual products. We have also referred to how the label Sony and the name Walkman were adopted with the aim of being 'global' brands.

Throughout the 1980s two important developments indicate how Sony began actively extending this and presenting the company as a 'global' corporation. First, the company aimed to operate in 'all' markets across the world, to reach as many potential consumers as possible. Second, the company aimed to reorganize processes of production in such a way so that they would not be limited by the constraints of the nation-state. In this case, a particular concern was how the effectiveness and international competitiveness of Japanese companies were constrained by the value of the Japanese yen. This meant that goods produced in Japan were more expensive when exported and in competition with those made in other parts of the world.

To pursue these aims, Sony adopted a strategy of globalization that involved moving their manufacturing and marketing operations to different locations around the world and setting up 'local' operations in various countries. Such activities are closely related to another concept that has been part of discussions of globalization, that of global–local relationships. Globalization is here associated with dynamics of 're-localization', what Kevin Robins (1991) has called a 'new **global–local nexus**'. Robins has used this concept to point out how national conditions of production have become less relevant to the operations of major corporations who have become more concerned with establishing specific 'global–local' relationships. The global–local nexus becomes important for large corporations who attempt to establish a presence in a variety of strategically important localities around the world. Here we give an indication of the technological, financial and political reasons why Sony are doing this.

global–local nexus

We have already referred to how Sony faced problems due to the high value of the yen and the cost of Japan's secure 'life-time' employment system which meant that manufacturing in Japan was increasingly expensive. In addition to this, many of Sony's competitors were producing consumer technologies in parts of the world where workers were poorly paid and had few employment rights. One motive for Sony to move its manufacturing operations was a straightforward attempt to follow suit and reduce labour costs. Although the first Walkmans were manufactured and assembled in Japan so that the company's management could be close to operations and make any necessary modifications, once up and running, and not requiring so many modifications, additional assembly factories were established in Malaysia and Taiwan.

A further reason for moving assembly and manufacturing plants to other localities was technological. When producing televisions and radios the company needed to produce equipment that could receive broadcast radio waves in particular territories. These waves could not be artificially simulated in the laboratory and at one time the company had solved this by recording hours of broadcast waves on tape and then transporting them to Tokyo where engineers could tune in the equipment and make any modifications.

However, the company began to gradually move operations so that they could respond directly to local conditions. So, for example, Teletext was developed on site in the UK and Trinitron television was developed 'locally' in France. These arrangements meant that engineers could tune in the equipment and make any necessary modifications without all the previous toing-and-froing between one part of the world and Japan.

An additional practical consideration was that, by establishing and presenting themselves as a local company, Sony could use various national and pan-regional rules and regulations to gain the most appropriate and cost-effective environment to manufacture and produce its products. The company could exploit cheap labour in Malaysia, take advantage of grants that were available to attract new electronic industries into areas of industrial decline in the UK and lobby politically to influence regulations in specific parts of the world as a 'local' rather than a 'foreign' company.

Akio Morita has often referred to these various dynamics of the 'global–local nexus' as a process of 'global–localization'. This he has presented rather benignly as a policy in which the company makes use of local talent whilst being sensitive to local cultural differences. As the London *Evening Standard* newspaper once reported, a 'caring' and 'close involvement with staff and community in Britain' has been part of Sony's policy for many years (29 October 1992). In addition to 'caring for the community', Sony has frequently presented 'global–localization' as involving 'decentralized management' – a practice of devolving 'investment decisions, research and development, product planning and marketing' to enable local people to do things 'on the spot' (Cope, 1990).

No doubt Sony has improved the tuning of broadcast technologies and got closer to local markets. But for some staff this has not necessarily involved large degrees of local autonomy. Despite the abstract and universal significations of the term, the 'global' still has an identifiable headquarters that continues to exert a large degree of control, particularly over budgets and financial decisions. When Rainer Kurr, the general manager of Sony's European television operation, publicly stated that this was so and that Sony's factories were still controlled from Tokyo, he was promptly removed from his post (Barnet and Cavanagh, 1994, p. 66). The dynamics of the 'global–local nexus' which we have discussed here seem to involve the global as a dominant place (Tokyo) and the local as a dependent place (the UK, France or Germany).

At the same time that Sony began presenting itself as a 'global' company, staff also began to speak of **synergy**. This term was employed to refer to a strategy, adopted by many hardware and software producing companies, of attempting to synchronize and actively forge connections between directly related technologies and areas of entertainment. Sony's annual reports and advertising began to refer to the organization as a 'total entertainment company'. Sony was no longer simply a manufacturer of technological hardware, it was an integral part of a 'culture industry'.

synergy

4.3   Combining hardware and software: the culture industry

culture industy

The term **culture industry** was introduced by Max Horkheimer and Theodor Adorno (1979/1947) in the 1940s at a time when proposing such a connection linking culture with industry was a challenge to those who believed that the arts were independent of industry and commerce. Horkheimer and Adorno argued that under the capitalist system of production a 'culture industry' had been established in which industrial manufacturing, commerce and artistic endeavour had been fused in such a way that there was little difference between companies producing hit songs or movies and the industries that manufactured vast quantities of mass-produced foods, clothing and automobiles. What Horkheimer and Adorno were doing was connecting the idea of industry to culture to make the point that the growth of cultural production (with the advent of wireless, films and phonographs) was drawing on methods adopted and used in industrial manufacturing. (This issue is pursued further in **du Gay**, ed., 1997.) Since the time Horkheimer and Adorno were writing, the idea of the culture industry has undergone something of a shift. From applying the idea of industry to culture, theorists and indeed those involved in the respective companies have been applying the concept of culture to industry. Hence, whilst cultural production is 'industrial', so too is industrial manufacturing 'cultural'. As we have seen, for Sony, doing business has always involved practices of representation – concerning its products, its working practices and so on. This is one of the points we have sought to emphasize in this section on production and design.

However, there is a further way in which Sony has been playing a part in fusing previously separate ideas about culture and industry – through the strategy of *media synergy*. The idea of synergy came partly from an acknowledgement that Sony's Walkman was useless without the cassettes that were inserted into it, which in turn were useless without the musical recordings which they contain. Likewise, Sony's compact disc was useless without the music of recording artists, and the company's Betamax videocassette-recorder (no matter how technologically brilliant) was useless without videocassettes of films and music.

To pursue such synergies, Sony made a decision to gain access to music and films by acquiring a record label and a film studio. This strategy would provide the company with a cultural repertoire which would be available for the instant marketing of future technologies. The thinking that motivated such a move was that Sony would no longer have to engage in long negotiations to persuade film and record producers to market sounds and images on Sony's equipment. Instead, one company – Sony – could synchronize both processes. This again took Sony to the United States. In 1988 Sony built on their twenty-year relationship with the US record and entertainment corporation, CBS, in Japan by acquiring the record company outright and in 1989 Sony purchased Columbia Studios. Such a convergence was by no means as easy to manage as the company first envisaged and continues to be a source of antagonism within the company. (This will be explored in greater detail in **du Gay**, ed., 1997.) But here it highlights how text and technology, hardware and software, production and use are dependent upon each other and are interrelated: Sony is not simply a hardware company but part of a culture industry. It is producing both technological products and cultural forms; cultural products are produced via an industrial process and it is also an industrial company with a distinct company culture.

So far, we have tried to untangle some of these connections whereby culture and industry become interwoven in the production of modern entertainment technologies. We began by introducing you to an approach for carrying out a study of the culture industries by indicating how you need to think about both the production of culture and the culture of production. Through the Walkman story, we have shown how analysing production involves not only understanding how something is produced technically, but how that artefact is produced culturally – how the processes of production are represented in different ways. We considered how the Walkman's production was represented in distinct ways: as the activity of inspired individuals, the unique organizational culture of the company and as a happy accident at work. We saw how the identity of Sony as a company was continually created and re-created through these different representations, extending our earlier discussion of individual identities to that of corporate identities. We also highlighted some of the particular ways in which production is connected to consumption, how two key moments in the cultural circuit are made to articulate and hence brought together. However, such articulations should not lead to the conclusion that there is a simple 'fit' between production and consumption. There is no such stable and easy correspondence, as we shall discuss in the following section.

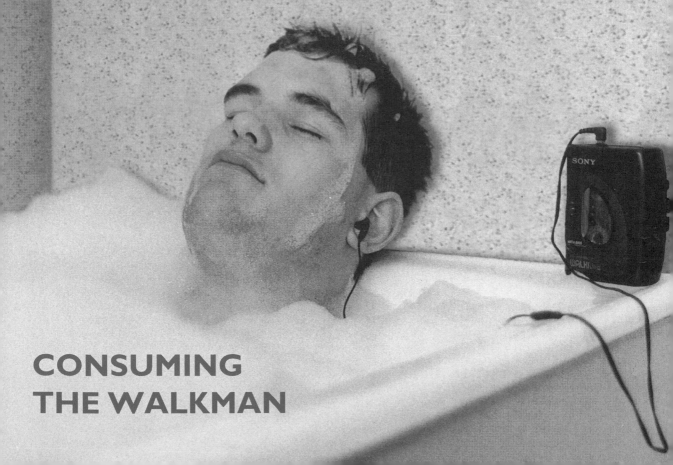

CONSUMING
THE WALKMAN

5.1   Introduction

It may be tempting to think that, once the Walkman leaves the factories and offices in which it is produced and enters shops and stores for purchase, there is little left to say concerning its meaning. After all, given that we have already seen how particular cultural meanings are ascribed to the artefact throughout its production process – whether this be in the form of those design practices examined in section 3 or those representational 'imaging' practices that were discussed at the beginning of the book – surely there can be nothing more to say about the Walkman as a material artefact?

If this is your initial reaction then you will not find yourself alone. For the longest time social scientists in general and sociologists in particular have assumed that processes of production of goods and services hold the key to understanding their social and cultural meaning. In this view 'production' dominates social life to such an extent that the constitution of all other domains of existence – the family and domestic relations, education and so forth – is in the final analysis determined by the productive 'base'.

This excessive focus on production and the economic has the effect of shutting down the analysis of culture, for it assumes that any meanings pertaining to artefacts or activities outside the sphere of production are by their very nature of a lower order and hence are unworthy of serious academic consideration. This seems a rather patronizing position to adopt, not least because one of the objectives of social science is to learn something of value from the practices of the people one is studying. One is most unlikely to learn anything from people's everyday practices if one approaches them with the view that they are unworthy of serious study because they are superficial and inauthentic substitutes for a denied alternative existence.

Such a strongly 'objectivized' view, with its antipathy towards any notion of human agency, seems unlikely to be able to tell us very much about what people make or do with material cultural artefacts, such as the Walkman, once they leave the factories and offices in which they are produced and imbued with particular meanings. Do those meanings change through the use people make of the Walkman ? If so, how and why and with what consequences?

These are the sorts of questions we will be exploring in this section which examines the role of practices of **consumption** in the production of meaning. This focus on consumption has two main purposes.   consumption

First, it serves to introduce you to another crucial element in our cultural circuit (see the Introduction to this volume). As was suggested above, it is not possible simply to 'read off' the meanings that material cultural artefacts come to have from their processes of production, no matter how crucial those may be. To do so is to impose an artificial closure on the biography of that artefact. For one thing, it fails to tell us how that artefact is used in social relations and what significance it obtains as a consequence of this usage.

As our notion of the cultural circuit suggests, meaning-making is an ongoing *process*. It does not end at a pre-ordained place. No doubt, the producers of material cultural goods and services wish it did and that they could establish its boundaries! However, that they cannot is evidenced by their dependence upon the techniques of cultural mediation outlined earlier – namely, design, marketing and advertising. After all, if consumption was simply a reflex of production, what need would there be for design, advertising or marketing expertise? There would be no need for the persuading role that these occupations provide if consumers were passive dupes who followed to the letter a script written for them by producers. As the social theorist Michel Foucault (1982) has argued, 'power' can only be exercised where there is freedom and hence a degree of uncertainty in any relationship. The fact that producers do not completely dominate or 'control' consumers but must ceaselessly attempt to exercise power over them, is attested to by the use they make of design, marketing and advertising in trying to create meanings for products with which consumers will identify.

To focus on practices of consumption, then, is to explore a crucial element in the process of meaning-making that lies at the heart of conducting a cultural study. No serious cultural study of the Walkman could afford to ignore exploring the ways in which that material cultural artefact has been used to make meaning by people in the practice of their everyday lives. A focus on practices of consumption therefore helps us to understand that meanings are not simply sent by producers and received by consumers but are always *made in usage*.

However, a focus on consumption not only extends the explanatory reach of our cultural study of the Walkman, taking us to another point on our circuit. It also introduces us to some of the most important theoretical debates currently being conducted within sociology and cultural studies. The second purpose of this section is therefore to give you a taste of some of the conceptions and theorizations of consumption currently circulating within sociology and cultural studies and to indicate to you some of the ways in which they challenge existing understandings of contemporary culture and society. As the term 'taste' suggests, these discussions are not intended to provide you with a comprehensive introduction to theories of consumption. Rather, they are designed to highlight briefly an important area of theorizing and research and to outline some of the concepts and issues associated with it that you will explore both more extensively and more intensively later on in the series. We begin by taking a closer look at the term 'consumption' and some of the meanings that have traditionally been attached to it.

5.2   Perspectives on consumption

Whilst taking a brief look at some of the dominant meanings carried by the term 'consumption', it seems difficult to understand how it has become such an important explanatory device for sociologists analysing contemporary culture and society.

One of the most ubiquitous meanings of the term is found within classical economics. Within this discourse, consumption usually refers to the purchase of a product and its exchange-value, or 'price'. This is consumption as the purchase of an object in the expectation that it might be exchanged for something else at a later date. Individuals consume in this way when they buy a piece of property or an object – such as an antique – whose value is likely to increase over time. At the same time, economists also talk about consumption in terms of 'use-value'. Use-values are normally attributed to what is termed 'final consumption', as a good is used up (a meal is eaten) or as a service is delivered (a plane flight is taken). In this sense of the term, consumption is associated with the satisfaction of needs and wants.

However, as the cultural theorist Raymond Williams (1976) suggested, historically the term consumption has carried a number of other connotations. As he indicated, consumption has been associated with waste, with dissipation, with decay. Consumptive bodies, for example, are those wasting away through illness. In religious imagery we have the fires of hell consuming the bodies of the damned. Consumption here has a series of distinctly pejorative connotations.

So how do we get from these economistic and medico-moralistic conceptions of consumption to contemporary sociological conceptions of consumption as the production of meaning through usage? The short answer to this question is that the distinctively cultural meaning of consumption has emerged both *through* and *against* these traditional definitions of the term. What we mean by this is that these particular conceptions have provided a *reference point* in relation to which contemporary meanings of the term consumption in sociology and cultural studies have been constituted.

This is best exemplified by turning to one of the first and foremost bodies of theoretical work on consumption and consumer culture to have emerged within the social sciences – what we will term 'the production of consumption' perspective.

5.2.1   The production of consumption

Proponents of this perspective – most commonly associated with the work of members of the Institute for Social Research and their disciples, known as the Frankfurt School (Adorno, 1991; Horkheimer and Adorno, 1979/1947; Marcuse, 1964) – argue that the expansion of commodity production throughout the twentieth century has given rise to a vast accumulation of material culture in the form of consumer goods, as well as to the proliferation of sites for purchase and consumption. This is deemed to have resulted in the growing importance of leisure and consumption activities in modern western societies and this in turn is regarded as increasing the capacity for ideological control, domination and manipulation of the population and thus their separation from an alternative and indeed more 'authentic' social existence.

According to the German social theorists Max Horkheimer and Theodor Adorno (1979/1947), for example, the same commodity logic and instrumental rationality manifest in the productive apparatus now saturates all other realms of existence. Leisure pursuits, the arts, and culture more generally, become part of an increasingly ubiquitous 'culture industry' (see section 4 above). In their discourse, the latter term is far from purely descriptive. For Horkheimer and Adorno the terms 'culture' and 'industry' had very different meanings, the former possessing connotations of refinement, learning and aesthetic contemplation, the latter tainted by the evils of capitalism. Their linkage, Horkheimer and Adorno argued, leads inexorably to the pollution of the 'higher' values of the world of culture by the debasing logics of production, the market and exchange and to the emergence of a standardized, homogenized 'mass culture' in which the market consumes everything of value in its path. In this process, citizens are turned into a passive mass of consumers, while culture ceases to stand in a critical relation to everyday life and becomes reduced to banal mass entertainment and amusement aimed at the lowest common denominator. In this world of mass culture, all is false and inauthentic because it is tainted by the hand of production, commodification and exchange.

As we can see, this perspective on consumption views it as thoroughly saturated and determined by the logic of capitalist production. On the positive side this at least has the effect of concentrating the mind on the increasingly commodified nature of material cultural artefacts, on the growth of large industrial organizations devoted to the production and distribution of commodified cultural goods and services, and the increasingly important role of consumption in people's everyday lives. However, these basic insights are accompanied by a number of problems. First, because production is represented as determining consumption, there is no space for human agency within this perspective. Consumer desires and needs, it is argued, are created by producers, with the assistance of their 'servants of power' and 'hidden persuaders'– the advertisers – and then satisfied by those same producers. Consumers, it would appear, are literally created by producers and then simply do their beckoning as if on automatic pilot.

Secondly, all mass-produced cultural forms are represented as superficial and inauthentic. In contrast to the mass 'popular' cultural forms produced by the 'culture industry' which are deemed to debase their users, the 'higher' arts of 'literature', opera and classical music are represented as ennobling 'true' culture. Because mass cultural artefacts are also commodities, their meaning is taken as given and immutable. The object has an 'essential' meaning determined by its commodified form. That meaning is necessarily 'negative' because of the nature of the production of that object – its association with capitalism. Produced by 'alienated' wage labour, commodities must always be sources of further misery, standing outside and against the citizen, offering lower-order pleasures for a denied existence. Underlying this critique is the idea that the desire to consume is a 'false' need created by producers and advertisers simply to sell more commodities, and is able to offer only delusory satisfactions.

It is interesting to note how this perspective on consumption relates to the economic and medico-moralistic conceptions we looked at earlier. As we argued above, sociological conceptions of consumption have developed both through and against these two conceptions. In the case of the present perspective it is possible to delineate a debt to both conceptions. On the one hand, the proponents of the 'production of consumption' perspective treat consumption simply as a matter of economic exchange and utility. Consumption in this sense concerns the growing dominance of instrumental rationality in all areas of life (where the value of everything is measured exclusively as a means to a calculated end), to the point where all differences, cultural traditions and qualities become transformed into quantities. On the other hand, there are also distinct traces of the medico-moralistic conception of consumption in this perspective too. This is most apparent in the opposition constructed between 'real' and 'false' needs. The assumption appears to be that, because people are not able to express themselves through their labour, which is represented as the 'real' authentic site of human self-creation, they have to seek compensation in the 'false' pleasures of consumption. Consumption in this sense eats away at their real selves – just like a consumptive illness – turning them progressively into pathologized, dehumanized 'happy robots' (Mills, 1951).

As we mentioned earlier, the 'production of consumption' perspective, with its objectivist, élitist and rather patronizing stance, has had considerable influence in framing the interpretation of consumption within the social sciences. However, its reach has been rather more extensive than that. As the social anthropologist Daniel Miller (1987, pp. 166–7) has argued, the production of consumption perspective, or what he terms the 'mass culture critique', belongs to that branch of conservatism which regards other periods in history, particularly the pre-industrial, as 'authentic' but the present as the final 'inauthentic' state. This strain of conservatism is not the exclusive property of either left or right, emerging as it does in the work of a range of diverse authors.

5.2.2 The Walkman and the production of consumption critique

Given its pervasiveness both within and beyond the academy, it should come as no surprise to learn that 'production of consumption' perspective has played a crucial role in structuring public debate about the social and cultural significance of the Walkman. Dire warnings about its negative socio-cultural effects have accompanied the Walkman ever since it first appeared in the public domain. Two recurring themes are worth noting. The first concerns the question of 'needs'. Many of the popular critical articles that appeared shortly after the Walkman was launched were concerned with highlighting the inherent 'uselessness' of the object and stressing that nobody actually 'needed' this technology. Second, and relatedly, the Walkman was criticized for its anti-social, atomizing effects. This strand of critique centred on the fact that the Walkman allowed individuals to switch off from the world as and when they liked and that this was likely to make them more introverted, self-serving and less tolerant of other people and of 'society' more generally. Let us examine each of these in turn, to see if we can delineate within them the presence of any of the key arguments and assumptions of the production of consumption critique.

As was shown in section 2, corporate managers at Sony were far from certain that the Walkman would be a success when it was launched because they did not believe there was a 'need' amongst consumers for a portable cassette-player without a recording facility. Although we need to be wary about the claim of the former head of Sony, Akio Morita (1987, pp. 79–80), that his 'instincts' told him the product would be a success, it is interesting to note that he considered his colleagues to be focusing too much on the technical details of the product and not enough on the ways in which people, particularly the target market of young people, actually consumed music in their everyday lives. And despite the original corporate legend that Sony did no 'market research' prior to the launch of the product, it is gradually becoming clearer, as was seen earlier, that the company did engage in some quite detailed research with young people to find out what they made of and did with the Walkman when they were given it; this in turn influenced both the design of the product and the advertising campaigns that accompanied its launch (Kuroki, 1987; Ueyama, 1982; Dreyfack, 1981).

This example may help us to gain a handle on some of the debates about consumer 'needs' that broke when the Walkman entered the public domain. As we have mentioned, considerable media attention was devoted to the Walkman as its use became more widespread, and much was made of it as the ultimate 'gimmick' product – a tape-recorder that did not even record. This latter observation often served as a springboard for arguments concerning the 'false needs' of consumer society and the ability of corporations to encourage the spread of selfish hedonism and lack of civility amongst people (Wallin, 1986; Noll, 1987).

Like the senior managers at Sony in the above example, these observers could see no obvious 'need' for the Walkman. However, unlike those managers these commentators were not making a marketing point in a business context; rather, they were offering a moral critique of contemporary culture more generally. For them, the growing sales of the Walkman typified the substitution of 'real' human needs – most often represented in the language of religious spirituality or that of the natural environment – by the 'false' ones of mass consumerism. Through the manipulation of people's behaviour, it was argued, large corporations were encouraging people to go way beyond the 'natural' limits to their needs and to become locked into an ever more vicious cycle of repetitive gratification.

As we have already indicated, these sorts criticisms of mass consumption have a long history. However, it is particularly interesting to note how much in common they have with the criticisms of mass culture made by members of the Frankfurt School. For example, in his influential book entitled *One Dimensional Man* (1964), the critical theorist Herbert Marcuse used the notion of natural human 'needs' in his critique of consumer capitalism. He argued that 'true' needs were based in human biology and in the natural rhythms of human interaction, uninfluenced by the logics of modern consumer capitalism. 'False' needs, on the other hand, were not natural but manipulated or induced by producers, advertisers and marketers; they had no basis in nature.

In a critique of this 'production of consumption' perspective, Jean Baudrillard (1988) opposed the notion that needs are finite, natural or fixed to any particular objects and rejected the tendency to treat consumers as mere ciphers for the will of producers. Like Akio Morita, Baudrillard argued that meaning does not reside in an object but in how that object is used. Certainly, producers attempt to inscribe particular meanings into products, he argued (often, as we have seen, through research with consumers, seeing what they think about and do with those products), but that does not exhaust the meanings those objects may come to have when they are consumed. In this sense production and consumption are linked, but one does not determine the other. Baudrillard writes that the production of consumption perspective

> ... is forced to represent the individual as a completely passive victim of the system ... We are all aware of how consumers resist such a precise injunction, and of how they play with 'needs' on a keyboard of objects. We know that advertising is not omnipotent and at times produces opposite reactions; and we know that in relation to a single 'need', objects can be substituted for one another ... [I]f we acknowledge that a need is not a need for a particular object as much as it is a 'need' for difference (the desire for social meaning), only then will we understand that satisfaction can never be *fulfilled*, and consequently that there can never be a *definition* of needs.
> (Baudrillard, 1988, p. 45)

In contrast to the production of consumption perspective, Baudrillard argued that material culture does not simply, nor indeed primarily, have 'use' or 'exchange' value, but that it, more importantly, has 'identity' value. By this he means that the consumption of material culture is important not so much for the intrinsic satisfaction it might generate but for the way it acts as a marker of social and cultural difference and therefore as a communicator. For Baudrillard, consumption functions 'like a language':

> Consumption is a system of meaning like a language ... commodities and objects, like words ... constitute a global, arbitrary and coherent system of signs, a cultural system ... marketing, purchasing, sales, the acquisition of differentiated commodities and object/signs – all of these presently constitute our language, a code with which our entire society communicates and speaks of and to itself.
>
> (Baudrillard, 1988, p. 45)

Rather than being 'natural', needs are therefore 'cultural'. That is to say, needs are both defined and produced by the systems of meaning through which we make sense of the world and thus are open to being re-worked and transformed. In consumption, as in language more generally, usage changes or inflects the meaning of objects in particular ways and, over time, in different periods or contexts, and in relation to new situations, new meanings or inflections will emerge (see section 1). In this sense, the meanings that material cultural artefacts come to have cannot be fixed, since there is no way of insisting that the uses made of them and the meanings that usage produces will not change over time or in different contexts.

If you remember, there was also a second criticism made of the Walkman as its popularity grew. This particular criticism focused upon the Walkman as a

technology that could allow individuals to block out the world, literally to 'tune in and turn off'. (This issue will be explored in greater depth in section 6.) This was regarded as potentially dangerous because it could lead to increasing individualization and atomization of the population and to the erosion of public life. In the United States, for example, the conservative thinker Allan Bloom (1989) complained that the unity of national culture was being undermined by a turning away by students from the 'canon' of universally revered great works – Shakespeare, the Bible and so on – in favour of, in his opinion, a second-rate, pluralized curriculum. Bloom explicitly linked this 'closing of the American mind' with the atomized, distracted and uncivilized modes of personal conduct that the Walkman had engendered amongst young people: 'As long as they have the Walkman on', he argued, 'they cannot hear what the great tradition has to say.'

Bloom was not alone in chastising the Walkman for the damage it was inflicting on civic mores. Other guardians of public morality emerged with equally damning indictments of the technology and its effects. In an article in the US magazine *Christianity Today*, Mark Noll, a history professor from Wharton College, argued that the Walkman posed a serious threat to the future of Christianity, not only because it fed 'the hedonism that is the fate of America in the late twentieth century', but more importantly because it called 'into existence still one more competitor to the voice of God' (1987, pp. 22–3).

Once again, these criticisms assume in advance something both about the Walkman and the people who use it. 'Atomizing', 'distracting' and 'alienating' effects are 'read off' from some of the possibilities inherent within the technology – the fact that individuals can use it to listen privately in public spaces, for example – with little to no attention being paid to exploring how the Walkman is being actively used in everyday socio-cultural practices and to what ends. In moves reminiscent of the 'production of consumption' perspective – particularly, in this case, the comments of Theodor Adorno (1991, pp. 40–4) on the 'regressive' effects of individual listening practices – these forms of criticism allocate a debasing influence to the technology as a consequence of its mass-produced, 'popular-cultural' status and contrast this with the presumed ennobling qualities of, in Bloom's case, 'high art' and, in Noll's case, Christianity.

Sony's own market research into Walkman usage offers some evidence with which we can analyse these claims. Sony divides usage into two particular types: 'escape' and 'enhancement'. The former dimension is most apparent in the way the Walkman has been used by people travelling to work on crowded/ noisy trains, tubes and buses, for example, in order to create some personal space in those environments. Quite how this usage is leading to the decline of civic mores is not entirely clear. Certainly, there is no evidence to suggest that this so-called 'privatized listening' is inherently 'distracting' for those engaging in it – though depending on the volume at which listening takes place it may be for those nearby (see section 6 for more about this particular feature of Walkman use). The massive growth of 'talking-book' tape-cassettes, for example, which has been directly attributed to the listening habits that Walkman use has fostered, suggests that rather than simply 'amusing themselves to death' on the train/bus/tube, at least a certain – and growing – number of Walkman listeners are actually tuning into Bloom's 'great tradition': a survey in *The Guardian* newspaper (11 February 1995) indicated that among the top-selling talking-books in the UK at the end of 1994 could be found such 'pulp fiction' classics as *Samuel Pepys' Diaries* and Homer's *The Iliad*, as well as foreign language tapes, exam study guides and so forth.

In terms of 'enhancement', Sony also found plenty of evidence of 'active' listening. Talking-books, for example, can obviously span the divide of both 'escape' and 'enhancement' dimensions, depending, of course, on what the listener is after. However, one of the most frequently discussed 'enhancement' effects of Walkman usage refers to the ways in which it allows music to become mobile and enables individuals to impose their own particular soundtrack on the surrounding aural environment (Hosokawa, 1984; Chambers, 1990). Rather than representing this latter practice as inherently passive and alienating, however, many Walkman users have spoken of it as an active, creative practice which enhances rather than diminishes their relationship to the external environment. One young woman, writing of her Walkman experiences for *The New Yorker Magazine*, makes just such a point when she says:

> I know how people who don't wear Walkman feel about the rest of us. I know because they ask me if I think its a good idea to wear headphones around, as if there might be something natural or wholesome about subjecting oneself to the cacophony of, say, a midtown sidewalk next to a construction site during rush hour. Once in a while when my batteries run low, I'm forced to hear what I've been missing, and, except for the occasional titillating snatch of conversation, I don't think it amounts to much. But when I'm listening to the Walkman I'm not just tuning out. I'm also tuning in a soundtrack for the scenery around me.

(1989, pp. 19–20)

This personal description of Walkman 'consumption' suggests the tactical character of its use. There is no grand 'universal' turning away from the world into privatized, atomistic distraction. The Walkman is used quite specifically (and only for a certain time-span) and there is no reason to assume that the user has slipped the reins of society. As the cultural theorist Ian Chambers, for example, has suggested, while on one level the Walkman may serve to set one apart, it also simultaneously reaffirms 'individual contact to certain common ... measures (music, fashion ... metropolitan life)' (1990, p. 2). In this sense Walkman use is still a *social* practice because, while one's listening may be private, the codes that inform that listening are inherently social – musical genres and fashion, for example. In other words, while listening privately in public, one is still socially connected in important ways.

Rather than assuming in advance that the Walkman has a preordained meaning and reading off cultural, social and political effects from these assumed meanings, what these and other examples highlight is the importance of exploring the different uses made of the Walkman in the practices of their everyday lives by different sorts of people in different contexts.

To round off this part of the section, we would like you to read an extract from an article by the cultural theorist Rey Chow. In this piece Chow explores some of the cultural and political implications of the recent appropriation of the Walkman by Chinese youth groups. This is a not an easy piece to read but do not panic if you wonder what it is all about. It is difficult, in part, because it is written in a style with which you may not be entirely familiar or comfortable.

READING F

Now turn to the Selected Readings at the end of the book and read 'Listening otherwise, music miniaturized: a different type of question about revolution', by Rey Chow.

Try reading it a couple of times, taking notes as you do so. Bear in mind the following questions:

1   Why does Chow interpret 'distracted' forms of listening as important symbolic acts in the Chinese context?

2   In what sense does use of the Walkman in China have political connotations that simply are not available in the West?

A central argument of Chow's text is its demand that we examine practices of consumption in their specific contexts and not allocate 'universal' meanings to those practices in advance of such an examination. She argues that some of the concepts deployed by the Frankfurt School scholars – such as 'distraction' – can be applied to practices of consuming popular music in China, but that these concepts have a completely different cultural meaning in the Chinese context. As she argues, for the Frankfurt School, concepts such as 'distraction' must be interpreted negatively. For this school of thought, cultural products which do not attract their audience's entire attention were indicative of capitalism's alienating and pacifying effects on people. For Chow, on the other hand, contemporary Chinese popular music which does not invite a fully concentrated response from its listeners acts as a form of protest against the Chinese communist authorities. In contrast to the 'official', grand music of the Chinese state, which Chow says aims to reinforce 'a kind of obligatory cultural memory in which the founding deeds of communist ancestors are properly honoured' and which requires intense, concentrated public listening, Chinese popular music is banal. However, in the context of this officially sanctioned, grand, collective music, banality is dangerous and hence not banal at all.

Similarly, she argues that in a society where the *only* acceptable mode of listening is public, Walkman usage has distinctly political implications. In a complete overturning of Frankfurt School assumptions about consumption, Chow argues that the mobile private listening that Walkman-use effects is empowering for Chinese youth because it allows them 'to be deaf to the loudspeakers of history' in public. In China, she says, 'listening is not as Adorno describes popular music in America, "a training course in … passivity", rather it is a "silent" sabotage of the collectivist demands of the Chinese state.'

What Chow's arguments, along with those other criticisms of the 'production of consumption' perspective outlined above, attest to is the importance of not assuming that meaning resides in an object outside of how that object is used and that meaning can therefore never be altered. Consumption from the latter perspective must always be passive because it simply involves consumers following a pre-written script. What we have argued, however, is that, while particular products are inscribed with meaning in their production, they are not the only meanings that those products may come to have. In order to do a cultural study, we must pay attention to the ways in which products are consumed and the meanings that come to be attached to objects through those processes of consumption.

5.2.3 Consumption as socio-cultural differentiation

As the work of Chow indicates, practices of consumption are much more varied than the 'production of consumption' perspective ever dreamt of. As we have seen, individuals and groups do not respond in a uniform and homogeneous manner to the material culture with which they are confronted. Rather their consumption of commodities is highly differentiated. However, as Baudrillard's comments above suggest, practices of consumption may be differentiated but they are by no means 'random'. For if commodities have social importance as signs and symbols – if they have what we termed above 'identity value' – then this suggests that practices of consumption and the meanings they produce are *socially structured*. This in turn suggests that to speak of 'consumption' in a general sense serves to gloss over the very different activities that are encompassed by the term and the ways in which different sorts of people – for example, men and women, rich and poor people in different societies – are situated differently in relation to those activities.

In this section we will briefly examine the ways in which Walkman usage is socially structured and explore the ways in which consumption of this artefact serves to mark social difference.

The suggestion that consumption activities are linked to patterns of **social differentiation** is not new. In his classic study of the 'conspicuous consumption' of the *nouveaux riches*, *The Theory of the Leisure Class*, the sociologist Thorstein Veblen (1957/1899) argued that the consumption of goods acted as a primary index of social status. Although Veblen was particularly interested in outlining the ways in which the leisure class

social differentiation

expressed their status through distancing themselves from the world of practical necessity and paid employment, he also suggested that no social group was entirely exempt from the practice of 'conspicuous consumption'. In other words, he argued that no matter how ostensibly poor people might be, their consumption practices always tend to have 'identity' value and not simply 'use' value. This point – that all consumption practices are *cultural* phenomena and not simply 'brute' *economic* phenomena – has been picked up and developed by the French sociologist Pierre Bourdieu (1984) in his wide-ranging examination of consumption and class in France.

According to Bourdieu, what we consume and how we consume always involve judgements on our behalf which at the same time identify and render classifiable our own particular judgement of taste to other people. He writes:

> Consumption is ... a stage in the process of communication, that is, an act of deciphering, decoding, which presupposes practical or explicit mastery of a cipher or code ... A work of art has meaning and interest only for someone who possesses the cultural competence, that is, the code, into which it is encoded ... taste classifies the classifier. Social subjects, classified by their classifications, distinguish themselves by the distinctions they make, between the beautiful and the ugly, the distinguished and the vulgar, in which their position in the objective classifications is expressed or betrayed.
>
> (Bourdieu, 1984, pp. 2, 6)

For Bourdieu, consumption is at one and the same time a material and a symbolic activity. It involves active discrimination through the purchase, use and evaluation of commodities and hence their construction as meaningful objects. Objects present themselves to us for consumption both as material and symbolic forms. Our capacity to consume them refers both to our social positioning materially – in terms of the financial resources at our disposal, for example – but also symbolically, in terms of the social dispositions and taken-for-granted assumptions, what Bourdieu terms our 'cultural capital', that is, the norms of conduct we learn through our family upbringing and educational training. We bring our cultural capital to bear on those objects in terms of their appropriateness for us as certain sorts of people.

habitus

For Bourdieu, consumption expresses taste, and taste lifestyle. All are in turn expressive of what he terms **habitus**. By this latter term, Bourdieu is referring to the unconscious dispositions, the classificatory schemes and taken-for-granted preferences which are evident in an individual's sense of the appropriateness and validity of his or her taste for cultural goods, and which not only operate at the level of everyday knowledge but are also inscribed onto the individual's body (see **Woodward**, ed., 1997). According to Bourdieu, different social classes can be seen to have a different habitus and hence to operate each with a distinct taste structure and 'lifestyle'.

Having indicated the ways in which taste for cultural goods functions as a marker for social class, Bourdieu goes on to map out the universe of taste and lifestyles – with its structured oppositions and finely graded distinctions – which operated within French society at a particular point in time (in this case the 1960s and 1970s). In the case of food consumption, for example, Bourdieu indicates that the working classes were found to prefer the immediacy and security of abundance: a plentiful table proclaiming itself to those around it, strong red meat, unpretentious red wine, and solid breads and cheeses. Middle-class food became 'cuisine'. Taste here was based on knowledge of the 'proper' methods of preparation and presentation, as well as on the 'correct' foodstuffs to eat for a well-balanced diet. In his discussion of the food consumption of the upper classes, Bourdieu distinguished between two different groups. The first, whom he termed the economically dominant 'fraction' of the upper classes, were found to prefer rich sauces and desserts, supplemented by rare and luxurious items such as vintage champagne and truffles. Meanwhile, the preferred food of what he termed the economically dominated but culturally dominant fraction of the upper classes was *nouvelle cuisine*, a meal in which considerations of aesthetic presentation were considered infinitely more important than any regard for sustenance.

In contrast to the view of a grey, conformist 'mass culture' in which the uses made of goods by consumers simply reflects the purposes inscribed into them by producers, Bourdieu indicates the ways in which particular constellations of consumption, taste and lifestyle practices are differentiated by social class. In so doing he indicates how consumption practices do not simply reflect class position but, more importantly, *how class difference is constructed through the consumption of goods*. However, despite its explanatory reach, there is none the less a number of criticisms that can be made of Bourdieu's analysis.

First, Bourdieu sees social class as the main determinant of consumer behaviour and social status. Although he did not intend to reduce his model of society to any single social attribute, it is none the less the case that he does not have as much to say about other major sources of social difference – age, gender and ethnicity, for example – which cut across and intersect with social class. At the same time, Bourdieu's representation of class as something 'objective' and given, and in the last instance explicable in terms of the relations of production, imposes a rather rigid and restricting framework on the analysis. In part, this 'static' aspect of his analysis is the product of the methodology he employs. Because Bourdieu explores consumption through the use of a highly structured questionnaire, he is only able to elicit quiescent responses from his research subjects, rather than insights into their everyday practices which he might have been able to obtain had he deployed a more qualitative methodology, such as participant observation. Rather than producing a dynamic picture of the interaction of 'structure' and 'agency' which Bourdieu (1989, p. 15) says was his aim, the subject of his work seems once again – like the subject of the production of consumption perspective – to be an unduly constrained and rather one-dimensional social actor.

For all its subtlety and sensitivity, Bourdieu's analysis, as the cultural theorist Michel de Certeau has argued, still assumes that consumption 'necessarily means "becoming similar to" what one absorbs, and not "making something similar" to what one is, making its one own, appropriating or reappropriating it' (1984, p. 166). In other words, because Bourdieu's analysis is largely based upon the mapping of differences between goods onto differences between social groups, and because the latter are treated as prior social divisions unaltered by these processes of consumption, people become unilaterally trapped in positions from which they are unable to extricate themselves. Therefore although Bourdieu indicates the importance of consumption to the production and reproduction of class divisions, he is unable to explain the ways in which consumer practices may crosscut given social divisions creating new social identities and differences in the process (see **Mackay**, ed., 1997).

5.2.4 Walkman consumption and social differentiation

As we have seen, Bourdieu uses a highly structured questionnaire to explore people's consumption practices. As Miller (1987) has indicated, this questionnaire is very similar to the sort of techniques that marketing companies use to track consumer behaviour in particular markets. Given this similarity of methodology, it may be useful to focus on a marketing survey specifically related to Walkman consumption in order to see if it can help us to articulate more clearly some of the benefits and pitfalls of Bourdieu's approach to analysing consumption.

ACTIVITY 6

You should now turn your attention to Table 5.1 and Figure 5.1. This table and bar-chart refer to the consumption of portable stereos in Britain in 1985 and 1991 and are derived from a marketing report compiled by the firm Mintel. You should examine them carefully, bearing in mind the following questions:

1   What appears to be the main social determinant of Walkman consumption?

2   Are any other social differences important factors in explaining consumption of the Walkman?

3   To your mind, what are the limitations of these data in explaining consumption of the Walkman?

There are a number of ways in which these data can help us to assess the explanatory reach of Bourdieu's analysis at the same time as giving us a picture of Walkman consumption in Britain.

The first thing that struck us in reading the table and chart was the importance of generational differences to consumption of the Walkman (remember the importance of generation in the advertisements analysed in section 1). Sony's corporate strategy vis-à-vis the Walkman seems vindicated here, in that their assumptions about the target market for the Walkman are matched by the actual consumption of their product. All the work they put into market research and in advertising the product in such a way as to appeal to young people appears to have paid off. As we can see from Table 5.1 and Figure 5.1, the Walkman is consumed most frequently by young people between the ages of 15 and 34, and most particularly by those between the ages of 15 and 19, where it is twice the national average. Overall, consumption of the product seems to decline with age.

Age is not the only important social difference that emerges from these tables, however. Gender, class and geography are also important factors in explaining

Walkman consumption. As you can see, men are more likely to own a Walkman than are women, though gender differences appear less marked than those of class and of roughly the same weight as those of geography. Overall, the picture that emerges of the 'typical' Walkman consumer is of a young man from a middle-class background – and hence more likely to be in employment than those in lower class groupings – living in the wealthier parts of the United Kingdom, namely London and the South East.

So, what can this brief examination of a marketing survey tell us about Bourdieu's survey approach to analysing consumption? Well, the first thing to note is that, had Bourdieu been looking particularly at the consumption of the Walkman, his privileging of class would have hampered the explanatory power of his analysis. As we have seen, if one particular attribute governs the logic of Walkman consumption it is not class but rather age. This lacuna in Bourdieu's schema might have been alleviated if he had paid attention to the meanings attached to objects during their production. However, he has little to say about the prior coding of objects in production. As we saw earlier, social class was not the most important factor for Sony in developing the Walkman. The company concentrated on young people as the target market throughout the production process, ensuring the product had a low price so that different sorts of youth – rich and poor, male and female – could have a chance to own it, and constructing advertising and other publicity materials which

FIGURE 5.1
Ownership of personal stereos by class, age and gender, 1985 and 1991.

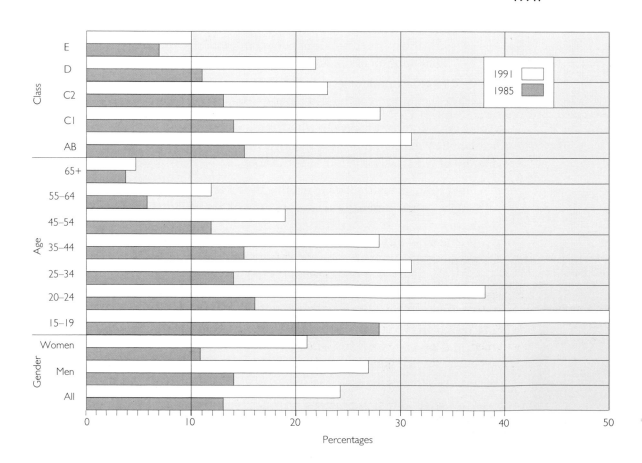

Percentages

TABLE 5.1 Ownership of personal and portable hi-fi amongst adults*, 1985 and 1991:
by gender, age, socio-economic grouping, home area, employment and marital/family status

		Portable radio/ cassette recorder		Portable cassette recorder		Portable radio		Personal stereo	
		1985 %	1991 %	1985 %	1991 %	1985 %	1991 %	1985 %	1991 %
Gender	All	31	33	24	16	42	35	13	24
	Men	34	34	26	17	44	37	14	27
	Women	29	31	22	15	40	33	11	21
Age	15–19	45	36	35	20	36	22	28	50
	20–24	39	36	22	16	33	21	16	38
	25–3	33	38	28	16	43	28	14	31
	35–44	34	37	33	19	46	36	15	28
	45–54	33	32	25	17	46	39	12	19
	55–64	27	30	19	16	46	46	6	12
	65+	16	24	12	12	40	44	4	5
Class	AB	36	40	31	20	54	47	15	31
	C1	34	37	26	18	47	37	14	28
	C2	33	32	24	16	40	32	13	23
	D	28	28	21	14	36	29	11	22
	E	20	24	17	11	32	30	7	10
ITV region	London/TVS	32	35	25	17	45	39	14	26
	Anglia/Central	31	33	23	16	42	36	12	24
	Harlech/TSW	31	33	23	16	42	36	12	24
	Yorkshire/ Tyne Tees	30	32	24	17	41	34	11	22
	Granada	30	34	23	16	39	32	12	23
	Scotland	30	31	27	15	39	29	14	23
Job status	Working	36	35	28	17	37	34	15	29
	Not working	27	30	21	15	40	36	11	18
Marital/ family status	Married	30	33	24	16	45	38	11	22
	Not married	33	32	24	16	45	38	11	22
	Children	35	36	32	19	41	30	16	31
	No children	28	31	20	15	42	38	11	20

Note: *Taken from annual survey of 24,651 adults in 1985 and 25,604 adults in 1991.
Source: TGI, BMRB 1985–91/Mintel.

represented young people as the main potential users and beneficiaries of the Walkman.

Another major problem for Bourdieu's methodology, and one it shares with survey techniques more generally, is that statistical tabulations can only tell us about who has bought what, not what meanings those products have for those buying them, nor how those products are used in the practices of everyday life. While far from useless, the survey can only paint a static, quantitative picture of who consumes what; it cannot offer a vibrant, qualitative picture of how something is consumed and what meanings are produced through those processes of consumption. As the cultural theorist Michel de Certeau has argued, the survey approach adopted by Bourdieu and utilized by producers too, can only count '*what* is used, not the *ways* of using. Paradoxically, the latter become invisible in the universe of codification' (1984, p. 35). Here de Certeau is suggesting that the survey method can only classify and tabulate the quantitative effects of consumption practices. It cannot represent nor pin down for analysis the practices themselves. The latter prove too slippery for quantitative techniques.

As de Certeau suggests, in relationship to quantitative analyses, practices of consumption 'circulate without being seen, discernible only through the objects they move about and erode'. What is missing here is any exploration of the practices of consumption through which youth groupings come to identify with and own the Walkman, or through which the Walkman is gendered in particular ways. What Bourdieu's survey cannot offer is much insight into these everyday consumer practices through which objects are given meaning. Hence only certain quantitative *economic and cultural after-effects* of those meaning-making processes are visible in his analysis.

5.2.5 Consumption as appropriation and resistance

If Bourdieu's work marks an important turn towards culture – in treating objects as both material and symbolic at the same time – in the analysis of consumption, his approach, as we have just seen, is not without its problems. In particular, as we indicated above, 'structure' appears to unduly constrain 'agency' in Bourdieu's work to the extent that the consumers who appear in it seem rather too passive.

The final approach to the analysis of consumption which we want to discuss is one that attempts to overcome both the pessimism of the production of consumption perspective and the objectivist tendencies inherent within accounts of consumption as social differentiation. This 'third way' concentrates its energies on exploring – most often, but not exclusively, through observing people 'in action', deploying what is known as the 'ethnographic' method – what individuals and groups make of and do with the objects they consume. In other words, this approach attempts to analyse how objects are made meaningful in the processes of their consumption.

Rather than viewing consumer behaviour as a simple expression of the will of producers, or of already existing, and seemingly immutable, social divisions, consumption in this perspective, as the cultural theorist Michel de Certeau (1984) suggests, can be conceived of as 'production' in its own right. He describes consumption as a productive activity because it leaves neither the person engaged in it, the object(s) involved, nor the sphere of production untouched. He argues that the meanings attached to – or coded into – objects in the act of their initial production are never automatically folded into the psychic life of those at whom they are aimed. Meaning, he argues, is also produced by consumers through the use to which they put those objects in the practice of their everyday lives. So while the 'elements' used may be determined in the sphere of production, how those are used – to what ends and with what effects – cannot be so easily pre-established.

As we mentioned earlier in this book, despite the enormous efforts made throughout the production process – through the use of design, advertising and marketing processes, for example – to create markets for given products, profits are always dependent upon the ability of producers to *interpret* the changes in meaning that products undergo throughout their consumption. In this sense, production and consumption are not completely separate spheres of existence but rather are mutually constitutive of one another. What happens to a product in consumption has effects for producers and so on, in an ongoing cycle of **commodification** – where producers make new products or different versions of old products as a result of consumers' activities – and **appropriation** – where consumers make those products meaningful, sometimes making them achieve a new 'register' of meaning that affects production in some way. In this sense, the meanings that products come to have are constructed in this process of *dialogue* – albeit rarely an equal one in terms of power relations – between production and consumption.

commodification

appropriation

One of the first attempts to articulate this gap between the lived practices of consumption of particular social groups, and the plans and programmes of powerful institutions can be found in the work of what has come to be known as 'subcultural analysis'. Focusing on the 'subcultural worlds' of mainly white, male, working-class youth, the studies of sociologists such as Paul Willis (1978) and Dick Hebdige (1979) emphasized the ways in which subcultural groupings – such as rockers, teddy-boys and punks – used commodities as signifiers in an active process of constructing 'oppositional' identities (see the Introduction to **Mackay**, ed., 1997). Through their symbolic work of 'consuming' material culture, these groups were seen to translate commodified objects from an 'alienable' (because linked to capitalist production) to an 'inalienable' condition, that is, from being an apparent symbol of estrangement (alienation at work) to being an artefact which symbolizes identity and 'belongingness' (as part of the culture of that group). Practices of consumption were therefore key elements in the production of an 'inalienable world' in which objects were firmly integrated into the development of particular social relations and group identity. 'Punk' culture, for example, involved the re-appropriation of 'banal' everyday items such as safety-pins and bin-liners through their translation into objects of personal adornment and display; this served to make a particular statement about their user's sense of identity in relationship to the conventions of 'mainstream' society and its values. Thus, 'subcultural' studies insisted that consumption was not a passive process, but an active one, involving the signifying practice which puts to use the 'polysemic quality of commodities' (that is, the possibility that multiple meanings can be attached to them) as signs.

More recently, the implications of this form of subcultural analysis have been developed into a thorough-going view of contemporary consumer culture as a self-conscious critique of traditional representations of 'mass consumption'. In this perspective the massive explosion in the range of goods available for consumption in modern western societies is seen to have led to a proliferation of lifestyles available for consumers to adopt. Increasingly, it is argued, all consumers are self-conscious 'cultural experts', whose intimate knowledge of consumer culture allows them a greater freedom to use commodities to become what they wish to be. In playing with the range of commodities available, it is argued, consumers style identities for themselves through their consumption practices which overturn or transgress established social divisions and which resist easy classification (Chambers, 1985; Fiske, 1989a, b).

Both 'subcultural analysis' and this more recent 'pleasures of consumption' thesis have involved not inconsiderable gains over both the 'structural pessimism' of the mass culture critique and over those theories that conceptualize consumption simply in terms of social differentiation. They have done this through, for example, insisting on seeing social subjects as active agents who play a crucial role in creating their own identities through consumption and in indicating how **bricolage** – literally the activity of self-consciously mixing and matching any disparate elements that may be to hand – can cut across given social divisions to produce new cultural identities.

bricolage

However, both these explorations of consumption also bear interpretative costs. In particular, as a number of critics have argued, from the quite plausible premise that consumption practices cannot be derived from or reduced to a mirror of production – that consumers make meanings in reception and do not simply 'receive' and 'ingest' sent messages – many studies conducted in this vein appear to end up disconnecting consumption *entirely* from the forces and relations of production.

Having rescued consumption from the pessimism of the mass culture critique, it is argued, these forms of cultural analysis end up inverting the errors of earlier accounts. Instead of representing consumer behaviour through an exclusively productionist frame, these accounts project a vision of consumption practices as inherently democratic and implicitly 'subversive'. As the cultural critic Judith Williamson (1986) has argued, the blatant populism of the 'pleasures of consumption' thesis leads to the virtual abandonment of any form of critical interrogation: *all* consumer behaviour becomes imbued with a romantic glow of creativity – what the sociologist

David Morley (1992) has called the 'don't worry, be happy' approach – leaving no room for questions of relative power between producers and consumers, of the very different capacities available to people to access consumer goods and services, and of the constraints differentially operating on the ability of individuals and groups to effectively make an object achieve a meaning radically different from that encoded in it by its producer.

We shall use an example in order to explore some of the explanatory strengths and weaknesses of the sorts of theorizing that these authors are criticizing. The one we have chosen relates directly to consumption of the Walkman.

READING G

Turn to the Selected Readings at the end of the book and read the extract entitled 'A miniature history of the Walkman' by Iain Chambers. The article from which this extract is taken represents Chambers' attempt to explain the popularity and cultural significance of the Walkman. You should read it carefully. As you do so, note down what you think are the main points that Chambers is making about the Walkman.

Do you agree with his interpretation of its cultural significance?

Are there any points arising from the discussions of consumption by the 'production of consumption' analysts or by Bourdieu that you would use to qualify any of Chambers' arguments?

How did you respond to reading the extract from Chambers' 'A miniature history of the Walkman'? It is quite tough-going, isn't it? Chambers does make a number of interesting points, though, and it is worth paying careful attention to his argument. The first thing he tells us is that the Walkman has played a crucial role in making music more mobile. However, unlike earlier developments in sound-carriage, such as the car radio and the ghetto-blaster, the Walkman offers a 'portable soundtrack' that is 'above all, an intensely private experience'. There seems little to disagree with there. Indeed, as we saw earlier, these comments echo those which other writers have made. However, Chambers goes on to make a number of points which conflict with some of the interpretations of the Walkman that we encountered earlier.

He suggests that the meaning of the Walkman lies in 'the extension of perceptive potential' it offers to people. What does he mean by this? Well, this comment is obviously linked to his assertion that significant socio-cultural changes are taking place in the world as a result of a major re-organization of time–space relations. By the term 'a world fragmenting' Chambers seems to be referring to the ways in which the electronic media destroy the specialness of place and time through their ability to 'lift out' particular signs, images and sounds from their local contexts and to recombine them across time and space in what Chambers terms a 'mutable collage'. This alters our perception of the world in some pretty basic ways. For example, electronic media such as television, radio, telephone and computer all redefine our experience of space and time by allowing distant events to intrude into our everyday consciousness and for our consciousness to be in some part organized in terms of awareness of them.

For Chambers, the Walkman plays a special role in changing people's perceptions or consciousness by enabling them to escape the confines of a particular ordering of the urban environment in terms of the difference between public and private space (this is a point to which we will return in the next section). Through this little technology, he argues, we are no longer bound to listen in a particular place. The Walkman breaks the sanctity of place – you can only listen to music in the home or some other officially designated 'place' – and allows you instead to impose 'your soundscape on the surrounding aural environment ... thereby domesticating the external world: for a moment, it can all be brought under the stop/start, fast forward, pause and rewind buttons.' It is apparent that this analysis of the Walkman is far from simply descriptive. For Chambers appears to be making a number of value judgements about the Walkman's 'political' effects at the same time.

It is apparent, for example, that Chambers views the Walkman as in some sense an 'empowering' or liberating technology in that it allows a person to escape the formal confines of the planned city – the City as the planners and builders have 'rationally' constructed it – with its own particular soundscape (noisy traffic, shops blasting canned music at all and sundry) and to impose their own narrative, 'a customized story and soundtrack' on the urban environment. Chambers sees this 'domestication' of the public sphere as a 'disturbing act' because it challenges the authority of the ordered, organized city. While obviously not 'political' in the formal big 'P' sense of that term – no politician can be found standing for election on a Walkman ticket – Chambers none the less feels that Walkman use has important small 'p' political effects because it resists established definitions of place and the forms of conduct that are associated with them. Thus, he contrasts a centralized, ordered, rational city where patterns of walking and listening are clearly regulated with the chaotic, pluralized soundscape which he regards the Walkman as helping to create. There is no doubt that this contrast is also a statement of preference. Chambers obviously sees the Walkman as a means of creating an urban environment 'of our making' in opposition to one imposed on us from above. Chambers' piece is deliberately provocative and we should bear this in mind when we seek to interrogate its claims.

Chambers raises some important issues about the effects of Walkman use. One of the most interesting points he discusses is the changed perception of the urban environment that the Walkman technology fosters and how this is related to wider economic and cultural shifts currently affecting western societies (for example, those processes collectively known as 'globalization' mentioned earlier in the discussion of the production of the Walkman). Of particular importance here is the blurring of the boundaries between public and private space to which electronic media such as the Walkman contribute.

More than one way to use a Walkman; more than one identity associated with Walkman use.

However, these undoubtedly important points are accompanied by some pretty grand and unqualified assertions about Walkman use about which we should be wary. We note that Chambers offers no evidence to back up some of his rather grandiose claims about the Walkman – for example, concerning its political potential to resist the rationality of the ordered metropolis. Given the 'political' significance that Chambers attributes to 'everyday practices', it is somewhat problematic that he singularly fails to provide us with any empirical evidence of actual Walkman usage and its effects. Had he done so, it seems likely that some of his other assertions would have been quite dramatically qualified. Bourdieu's work alerted us to the far from uniform nature of consumption activities and their effects and our own reading of a Walkman marketing survey indicated that Walkman use is a highly differentiated phenomenon. Chambers' rather frequent use of the pronoun 'we' therefore needs to be disaggregated. Not everyone has a Walkman, and different people in different contexts use it for different purposes and to differing effect. Insofar as there are actual Walkman users who approximate to the picture Chambers paints, then they would tend to be certain sorts of young people and it seems highly unlikely that in relation to Walkman use they occupy the same position as Chambers himself, either socially, culturally or generationally.

Chambers' failure to recognize the uneven and differentiated nature of Walkman use – what we might term, following the geographer Doreen Massey (1991), its 'power geometry' – is accompanied by another significant omission – a failure to comprehend the nature of the relationship between production and consumption. Chambers appears to endorse a binary opposition between 'production' and 'consumption'. However, as we have noted throughout this book, such a conception is extremely problematic. The sorts of uses of the Walkman that Chambers celebrates as 'political' and 'transgressive' – listening privately in public space, creating one's own soundtrack for the metropolis – were coded into the Walkman during its production. Rather than being opposed to the productionist definitions of Walkman use, the consumer practices Chambers to which refers have achieved a certain fit with them.

If the 'production of consumption' theorists discussed earlier can be accused of cultural pessimism and determinism because of their belief that mass culture was by its nature a 'bad' thing and that production logics determined consumption practices, then the opposite applies to the sort of analysis conducted by Chambers. Rather than an excessive pessimism and determinism, Chambers instead expresses an excessive populism and voluntarism. He seems to view the Walkman as an inherently good thing because he believes it to be empowering and liberating for individuals, providing them with a cultural tool for taking charge of their own lives. This argument is voluntarist because, for example, it fails to acknowledge the meanings attached to the Walkman during its production which structure its use in certain important ways. It is populist because it assumes, for example, that the Walkman has uniformly positive effects. However, because neither consumption generally nor consumption of the Walkman in particular are

FIGURE 5.2
The Sony
Walkman: there's
a revolution in the
streets.

uniform, what may be a 'positive' effect for one person or group may be a highly negative effect for a different individual or group. This uncritical populism fails to recognize the complex power geometry of Walkman use.

In the final section we will examine these questions of 'power geometry' in slightly more detail by exploring the ways in which consumption of the Walkman has thrown up some interesting questions about the regulation of culture.

REGULATING THE WALKMAN

6.1   The Walkman and questions of cultural regulation

Over the course of the last ten to fifteen years or so, public debate in many of the advanced western societies has often focused on questions concerning the impact and role of electronic media – such as television, video and computers – in transforming both society at large and the domestic sphere in particular. As the sociologist David Morley has argued, 'public discourse from governmental papers through business forecasting to popular journalism abounds with images of the increasingly privatized family, shut off from public life, turned in on itself, within a culture of … privatized leisure' (1994, p. 101).

In the United Kingdom this debate was conducted against the background of a major shift in cultural values brought about by the policies of successive Conservative administrations (see the Introduction to **Thompson**, ed., 1997). The latter, which – among many other things – sought to privilege the private provision and consumption of goods and services over collective provision and consumption, and to encourage the development of acquisitive and entrepreneurial forms of individual conduct among the populace at large, were seen to have fed the public's desire for individualized and privatized forms of leisure. For some commentators, the Walkman was the ultimate consumer commodity for the 'a-social, atomizing, individualizing tendencies' of the 'enterprise culture' – a technology that allowed the individual to 'turn off' the social world at will and to concentrate on their own pleasure (Gardner and Sheppard, 1989, p. 53).

It is important at this point to differentiate between two distinct notions of public and private. On the one hand, the terms 'public and private' often refer to two distinct spheres of the social – the public referring to the sphere of communal life, and the private to the realm of the personal and the domestic. On the other hand, the terms are also used to refer to two distinct ways of organizing the provision of goods and services, most notably in the contrast drawn between state bureaucracies and private markets. While there are obvious overlaps between these two notions of public and private in everyday life, for analytic purposes we intend to keep them separate. Due to constraints of space, we shall concentrate primarily on exploring the impact of electronic media such as the Walkman in *transforming the relationship between the communal and domestic spheres*, and will not simultaneously analyse the place of the Walkman in the changing relationship between the public and private *provision* of goods and services. In other words, our discussion of the Walkman and the culture of 'privatized leisure' is conducted without recourse to debates about the privatization of public goods and services and the acquisitive individualism of the 'enterprise culture' (the latter debates are discussed in more detail in **Thompson**, ed., 1997).

As the first of a rapidly expanding range of individualized consumer technologies to emerge during the 1980s – later ones included the camcorder and the mobile phone – the Walkman found itself at the centre of public debates about the impact and role of electronic media in shifting the relations between public and private worlds. Not only this, the Walkman was articulated to both utopian and dystopian visions of various kinds, being positioned as, on the one hand, the purveyor of choice and increased freedom for the individual and, on the other, as the destroyer of public life and community values. It was this latter representation, referred to earlier, that was the main focus of public debate.

While earlier electronic media such as radio and television had been similarly chastised for their privatizing effects by encouraging home-based consumption, the Walkman was different precisely because it allowed that privatized pleasure to be taken into the public domain. Whereas television and radio took viewing and listening out of the public sphere and deposited them into the domestic sphere, the Walkman went one better (or worse, depending on your point of view) by allowing private 'domestic' pleasures, now considered to be the province of the home, and let them loose on the streets. The fear soon arose that if everyone was doing their own thing in the public sphere, to what extent was that sphere any longer public? What would those people share with one another? Wouldn't society be reduced to little more than the aggregate of atomized individuals living in a particular geographical space? (Indeed, wouldn't the household become simply a place where isolated individuals shared a kitchen and a bathroom?)

Clearly, electronic media such as the Walkman play a fundamental role in connecting the private and public worlds. What we are interested in exploring in this section is the way in which the incorporation of the Walkman into ongoing socio-cultural relations served to reconstruct the relationship between these two domains, and the questions of cultural regulation that this raised.

6.2 The Walkman: the public and the private

public and private
spheres

In modern western societies one of the foremost material and symbolic divisions framing the organization of social life has been that between **public and private spheres**. As a number of commentators have argued, the public sphere is most often associated with the formal institutions of the state, with the rule of law and with the world of work and the economy, whereas the private domain is represented as the realm of the personal, the emotional and the domestic. This division between public and private, as many feminist scholars have indicated, has been and remains fundamentally gendered, with the public world of power and influence associated with men and the private sphere of domestic life with women.

As we mentioned, this division between public and private is both material – in that it denotes an opposition between physical spaces ('office' and 'home', for example) – and symbolic – in that these spaces are made to signify different things in relation to each other, the former signifying the universal, the collective and the rational, and the latter the particular, the emotional and the personal. In this way, a hierarchy of value is attached to the differences between these two spaces which prioritizes one over the other.

This historical prioritization of the public sphere and related marginalization of the private sphere have important consequences for our understanding of the debates surrounding the role and impact of electronic media such as the Walkman. For arguments about the effects of these technologies in privatizing leisure are also debates about the relative importance of these two spheres. There is often more than a hint of moralizing in some of the discussions about the growing importance of the home as a site of leisure, in part because of the unsavoury connotations associated with the private in relation to the public.

While the growth of the home as a leisure venue may have done little to alter the organization of gender relations both within and without the home – as the sociologists Cynthia Cockburn and Susan Ormerod (1993, p. 131), for example, have argued, if for men the home is predominantly the site of personal relations and recuperation from work, for women (including working women) it still tends to be primarily a site of domestic labour and only secondly a site of leisure – it has none the less meant that certain activities have become defined as 'private'. As a number of commentators have argued, the primary mode of film consumption, for example, is via television/video, and hence located in the home, rather than the cinema (Morley, 1994). Similarly, listening to music has become defined primarily as something that takes place privately, in the home, via radio and stereo systems, rather than primarily in the public domain (Negus, 1992).

It is in the context of the increasing importance of the domestic sphere and of privatized forms of cultural conduct – viewing, listening and so on – that the Walkman is such an ambiguous technology. For it can and is used in the home – for example, by members of high-density families living in relatively restricted domestic circumstances as a means of creating some personal space – but it is primarily designed and marketed for mobile private listening *in public*. It is this 'twist in the tale' that the Walkman imparts to the conventional story of 'privatization' which might account for the strong reactions it has engendered and the regulatory problems it has thrown up in its wake. In other words, while there has been a steady move away from mainly public to predominantly private modes of viewing and listening, the Walkman marks an important inversion of this process by *taking private listening into the public domain*.

6.3   Walkman use and the blurring of boundaries

As the cultural theorist Iain Chambers has suggested, by bringing what was conventionally conceived of as a private act – private listening – into public spaces, the Walkman disturbed the boundaries between the private and public worlds. He writes: 'its uncanny quality lies in its deliberate confusion of earlier boundaries, in its provocative appearance "out of place"' (1990, p. 3). The latter phrase 'out of place' is suggestive because it brings to mind the reactions people had on first seeing someone wandering down the street with a Walkman on. Because the combination of activities – listening to music and walking at the same time – seemed odd and the equipment involved – small cassette-player and headphones – was seemingly located in the wrong context, people's initial reaction was to think, 'There's something strange or not quite right about this' (Hosokawa, 1984, p. 176). As a reporter for the US magazine *Money* wrote in an article structured as a 'letter to a friend':

> When you were in New York last month you wondered why some glassy-eyed folks were walking around with headphones wired to little boxes hanging around their necks. Well, after you left, I asked around and learned that we were wrong – they're not members of some crazy new cult … [R]emember when our mothers used to tell us that there was a time and a place for everything? That's not always true anymore. Those little boxes are portable tape cassette players … It seems that you don't have to stay home to listen to your stereo these days.
>
> (Button, 1981, p. 104)

This idea that the Walkman was somehow 'out of place' suggests that its presence in the public domain somehow offended people's ideas about what sorts of activities belonged where. In sociological language we could say that the Walkman offended our sense of social order – that systematic classification of objects which divides them into good/bad, appropriate/ inappropriate and so forth. As we saw earlier during our discussion of representing the Walkman, objects never speak for themselves; the meaning they come to have is, rather, a product of how those objects are classified by us. The identity of an object depends on a way of classifying it and making it meaningful.

classificatory
system

The idea that objects only achieve meaning through their insertion within a particular **classificatory system** has a number of important consequences. First, taken-for-granted assumptions about the 'nature' and 'essence' of objects are immediately open to doubt if one accepts that the meaning of any object does not reside within the object itself but is a product of how that object is socially constructed through classification, language and representation (see section 1 above).

Secondly, any system of classification is a *system of differences* in which the meaning the various elements have is *relational*. In other words, objects have no meaning of themselves but only in relationship to other objects within the classificatory system. So, for example, the object 'sun' only gets to mean what it does in relation to the object 'moon', or the word 'mother' only means what it does because the words 'father', 'daughter' and 'son' also exist. As we saw earlier, the 'public domain' only means what it does in relation to another term, the 'private domain'. To be what it is, the 'public' must exclude that which it is not, and the excluded elements are what we term the 'private domain'. This probably seems awfully complicated but actually is quite simple. Everywhere you look you will see classification at work, drawing boundaries between what is appropriate and inappropriate. For example, would you happily sit down to dinner if there were a pair of muddy boots on the dining-table? Or would you willingly eat your lunch in the lavatory? If, as we suspect, you answer in the negative, then you have just been involved in an act of classification! For in our cultural context, that classificatory system which we know as 'hygiene' divides up the world in particular ways. In that system, dirt is represented as a form of pollution and in order to keep ourselves pure we must eradicate its polluting potential from our lives (see the Introduction to **Woodward**, ed., 1997).

According to the social anthropologist, Mary Douglas, any system of classification is an ordering and ordering requires the rejection of 'inappropriate elements' (1966, p. 35). If an order or systematic pattern is to be maintained, we must eject or exclude that which would challenge the pattern and its continuation. She writes:

> ... order implies restriction; from all possible materials a limited selection has been made and from all possible relations a limited set has been used. So disorder by implication is unlimited, no pattern has been realised in it, but its potential for patterning is indefinite. This is why, though we seek to create order, we do not simply condemn disorder. We recognise it is destructive to existing patterns; also that it has potentiality. It symbolises both danger and power.
>
> (Douglas, 1966, p. 94)

Following Douglas's comments, we can begin to see how the Walkman could represent a danger to the established classifications of public and private spheres. For, as we argued earlier, the Walkman took those elements associated with private listening and allowed them to leave their normal position within social space and to enter a domain where they were materially and symbolically 'out of place'. As we saw from some of the public debates referred to in section 5.2.2, the Walkman created something of a 'moral panic' when it appeared, precisely because of its transgression of established symbolic boundaries.

Keep your personal stereo *personal!*

If your stereo annoys other passengers you are contravening the bye-laws.

As Douglas's comments also suggest, when something achieves the status of being 'matter out of place', when people represent it as a threat to order and to established patterns of conduct, the common reaction is an attempt to exclude it, to reject it. This was certainly a reaction that confronted the Walkman. Such antagonisms have centred around Walkman use on the London Underground that London Transport has had to draw up regulations for appropriate Walkman noise-levels on public transport and to advertise warnings of the penalties to be incurred should passengers play their Walkmans too loudly. In a recent case on the British railway system, a youth who had insisted on playing his Walkman at top volume had so enraged his fellow passengers that he was forcibly evicted from the train on which he was travelling (luckily for him while it was standing at a station!) and was later taken to court and fined for breach of the peace (*Melody Maker*, 1994).

GO SOUTH YOUNG MAN

A BEAUTIFUL SOUTH FAN has been fined £200 and ordered to pay £100 court costs after playing the band's "Miaow" album at full volume on his personal stereo during a train journey, and refusing to turn it down after a complaint from a fellow passenger.

The fan, 21-year-old Andrew Dunn, told The Maker: "It was a condescending, office-type geezer who complained, and he was only 23. He asked me, in my view impolitely, to turn it down. It was making a negligible amount of noise, and he'd asked me politely I probably would have gone along with it. But I felt that I was in the right, and just because there happened to be transport police on the train, he went and informed them.

"I felt that I got stitched up in court. I was called 'irritable and threatening' – but when the police was asked, 'In what way was Mr Dunn irritable and threatening?', he said,

'Well, he didn't actually say anything, but we just got that general idea.' So it comes out in all the papers that that's the way I am.

"The papers also said that I was arrested and thrown off the train. I wasn't. I was charged, and then left the train at my expected destination.

"When I played the tape in court at full volume, none of the witnesses would accept that that was they'd heard on the day, so again, I got stitched up."

[...]

Dunn does not intend to appeal, as he feels he would have little chance of winning. However, it now appears that The Beautiful South's label Go! Discs may come to his rescue. A spokesman for the company told The Maker last week that the label was considering paying the fine and costs.

Source:
Melody Maker,
17 September
1994, p. 6.

READING H

Now turn to the Selected Readings at the end of the book and read 'Menace II society' by Vincent Jackson.

As you will have gathered, this is a piece of journalism that describes one young person's experience of wearing his Walkman on the London Underground and the reaction this usage engenders amongst his fellow passengers. It is not a theoretically conceived piece so you should have found it quite easy to read. We found it interesting because this young man's experience seems to bear out Mary Douglas's comments about how people react to matter 'out of place'. As you will have seen, the author describes the Walkman as the 'scourge of the modern-day traveller, the leper's bell'. These images of the Walkman-wearer as 'plague-carrier' fit precisely our description of the Walkman as an ambivalent technology bringing together two incompatibles – private listening pleasure and the public domain – and hence challenging established boundaries between the two spheres. As we argued earlier, the metaphors of dirt and pollution tend to accompany those objects which do not fit established symbolic orderings because they are seen to be dangerous and needing of exclusion. Walkman-listening, the author continues, like kissing in public, is something that seems to cast the persons doing it into the role of 'nutter' because they are engaging in what is commonly held to be a private activity – personal pleasuring – in public and thus to be transgressing the boundaries of what is considered appropriate contextual behaviour.

As Walkman use has become a more accepted feature of everyday life – largely by dint of the weight of numbers of people using this technology and the habituation this has engendered among the population more generally – so moral panics over the Walkman have diminished somewhat – often simply to pass on to the latest technologies such as those currently surrounding the mobile phone and the Internet. However, that the Walkman is still not accorded a secure home in the world, that it continues to occupy an ambivalent position between public and private, can be evidenced by simply gauging one's own reaction when someone close to you in a public place puts on those little headphones.

6.4   Summary of sections 5 and 6

In these sections we have travelled a long way. We began by stressing the importance of *consumption* to understanding the different meanings attached to the Walkman throughout its life-cycle. We indicated that it was impossible to appreciate the complex biography of a cultural artefact such as the Walkman without exploring the ways in which it was consumed. We then set out to explore consumption of the Walkman through an analysis of some of the central conceptualizations of consumption that have developed in the social and human sciences over recent years.

Our discussion of the 'production of consumption' perspective helped us to understand the importance of the Walkman as a commodity and the ways in which production and consumption are inextricably linked. However, as we saw, this perspective was of limited use in explaining the diverse meanings that consumers attach to the Walkman because it assumed that the only meaning attached to the object was that enshrined in it as a result of its production. Consumption from this perspective must always be a passive activity because it simply involves consumers following a pre-written script.

In section 5.2.3 we went on to explore the ways in which the Walkman is used by different social groups to distinguish themselves from one another. Through an examination of the work of Bourdieu we were able to chart the ways in which consumption was a highly differentiated rather than a uniform social process. We also saw that, despite Bourdieu's increased attention to the symbolic dimensions of consumption, his analysis still tended to be dominated by a rather bleak conception in which people simply reproduced their class position through their consumer activities. By comparing Bourdieu's methodology with that utilized by a marketing company researching the consumption of the Walkman, we showed how both could only offer a static picture of who consumes what, rather than a dynamic picture of how commodities are given meaning through their insertion into everyday social relations.

In section 5.2.5 we then took a look at a perspective on consumption that represented it as a predominantly active rather than passive process in which goods were translated from mere commodities into objects with meaningful connotations in light of the position they occupied within the cultural life of particular individuals and groups. In this perspective consumption was represented as a 'productive' activity because it involved people in making commodities meaningful through their use in the practice of their everyday lives. Although we argued that this focus on actual practices was a significant improvement on earlier approaches, we also expressed some worries over the ways in which some advocates of this perspective attributed a romantic notion of resistance to consumer activities and viewed them as entirely autonomous of processes of production.

Through an examination of Iain Chambers' discussion of the cultural and political significance of the Walkman, we argued that some proponents of consumption as appropriation had 'bent the stick' too far in the opposite direction in an effort to remedy the deficiencies of the 'production of consumption' perspective. We suggested that, in contrast to the excessive pessimism and determinism of the latter theorists, the work of Chambers and some other like-minded theorists was both excessively populist and voluntarist. In arguing this, we focused in particular on the ways in which they ended up entirely divorcing 'consumption' from 'production'. We highlighted this error in relationship to the very close fit achieved between the meanings coded into the Walkman by its producers and the activities of consumption that these theorists regarded as somehow expressing 'political' resistance to a 'dominant order'.

In this final section we have sought to assess the cultural significance of the Walkman in rather more measured terms than those provided by some of the proponents of consumption as resistance. We indicated the way in which the Walkman was positioned as the latest in a long line of technological innovations leading to the decline of the public sphere and the increasing privatization of cultural life. We have suggested that the Walkman's significance and the problems of regulation its use had thrown up were related to the way in which it broke with this logic of privatization in an important respect. We showed that, while viewing and listening had come to be seen as increasingly private activities conducted mainly in the home, the Walkman disrupted this process because it allowed private listening to be conducted in the public sphere.

Using the work of Mary Douglas, we examined the ways in which the Walkman broke with the established classifications of public and private space and how its status as 'matter out of place' – being both public and private at the same time and therefore neither simply public nor private – had led to attempts by some public bodies to regulate its usage. We ended the section by suggesting that although the Walkman was now firmly established as part of the modern soundscape, its ambivalence had not completely disappeared. Antagonisms still erupt from time to time around its hybrid status as a vehicle for private pleasuring in public space. Indeed, lest the idea of a 'circuit' be receding from your grasp, it is worth bearing in mind that Sony has not been unaware of the regulatory antagonisms in which the Walkman has been implicated. Through the medium of market research and other techniques of consumer surveillance, the company has, as ever, responded to these developments. For some time the headphones accompanying the Walkman were large instruments covering a considerable portion of the outer ear. Nowadays the headphones tend to be tiny, designed to be inserted partially inside the ear. It is no coincidence that these headphones emit less noise than the older versions. It seems that they began to appear about the time the Walkman started to receive adverse publicity concerning its role in inducing anti-social behaviour. Remember the circuit now?

References

ADORNO, T. W. (1991) *The Culture Industry: selected essays on mass culture*, (ed. J. M. Bernstein), London, Verso.

ALDERSEY-WILLIAMS, H. (1992) *Nationalism and Globalism in Design*, New York, Rizzoli.

ARNOLD, M. (1932) *Culture and Anarchy*, Cambridge, Cambridge University Press.

BANKS-SMITH, N. (1990) 'Turn on, tune in, sod you television', *The Guardian*, 20 June, p. 38.

BARNET, R. and CAVANAGH, J. (1994) *Global Dreams: imperial corporations and the new world order*, New York, Simon and Schuster.

BAUDRILLARD, J. (1988) *Selected Writings,* Cambridge, Polity Press.

BBC (1991) *Design Classics* (BBC2 television series), episode on 'The Walkman', British Broadcasting Corporation.

BENJAMIN, W. (1970) *Illuminations*, London, Collins/Fontana Books.

BLOOD, J. (1981) 'Portable tape sales jump but pricing and margins shrink', *Merchandising*, March.

BLOOM, A. (1989) *The Closing of the American Mind*, Harmondsworth, Penguin.

BORRUS, A. (1987) 'How Sony keeps the copycats scampering', *Business Week*, 1 June, p. 43.

BOURDIEU, P. (1984) *Distinction* (tr. R. Nice), London, Routledge.

BOURDIEU, P. (1989) 'Social space and symbolic power', *Sociological Theory*, Vol. 7, No. 1, pp. 14–25.

BUTTON, S. (1981) 'Tuning in to rappers', *Money*, July, pp. 104–6.

CHAMBERS, I. (1985) *Urban Rhythms,* Basingstoke, Macmillan.

CHAMBERS, I. (1990) 'A miniature history of the Walkman', *New Formations: a journal of culture/theory/politics*, No. 11, pp. 1–4.

CHAMBERS, I. (1993) *Migrancy, Culture and Identity*, London, Routledge.

CHOW, R. (1993) 'Listening otherwise, music minitiaturized: a different type of question about revolution' in During, S. (ed.) *The Cultural Studies Reader*, London, Routledge (first published in *Discourse*, Vol. 13, No. 1, Winter 1990–91).

CIEPLY, M. (1983) 'Sony's profitless prosperity', *Forbes*, 24 October, pp. 129–34.

COCKBURN, C. and ORMEROD, S. (1993) *Gender and Technology in the Making*, London, Sage.

COPE, N. (1990) 'Walkmen's global stride', *Business*, March, pp. 52–9.

CRUZ, J. and LEWIS, J. (eds) (1994) *Viewing, Reading, Listening: audiences and cultural reception*, Boulder, CO, Westview Press.

DE CERTEAU, M. (1984) *The Practice of Everyday Life*, London, University of California Press.

DOUGLAS, M. (1966) *Purity and Danger*, London, Routledge.

DREYFACK, M. (1981) 'Sony Walkman off to a running start', *Marketing and Media Decisions,* October, pp. 70–71, 168.

DU GAY, P. (ed.) (1997) *Production of Culture/Cultures of Production*, London, Sage/The Open University (Book 4 in this series).

ELGER, T. and SMITH, C. (1994) 'Introduction' and 'Global Japanization?' in Elger, T. and Smith, C. (eds) *Global Japanization? The transnational transformation of the labour process*, London, Routledge.

FINANCIAL WORLD (1980) 'The surge in Sony', 1 October, pp. 42–4.

FISKE, J. (1989a) *Understanding Popular Culture*, London, Unwin Hyman.

FISKE, J. (1989b) *Reading the Popular*, London, Unwin Hyman.

FOUCAULT, M. (1982) 'The subject and the power' in Dreyfus, H. L. and Robinson, P. (eds) *Michel Foucalt: beyond structuralism and hermeneutics*, Brighton, Harvester Press.

GARDNER, C. and SHEPPARD, J. (1989) *Consuming Passion: the rise of retail culture*, London, Unwin Hyman.

GIDDENS, A. (1990) *The Consequences of Modernity*, Cambridge, Polity Press.

GLUCKSMANN, M. (1990) *Women Assemble*, London, Routledge.

THE GUARDIAN (1995) 'Switch on and listen', 11 February.

HALL, S. (1991) 'Old and new identities, old and new ethnicities' in King, A. (ed.) *Culture, Globalization and the World System*, Basingstoke, Macmillan.

HALL, S. (1996) 'On postmodernism and articulation' in Morley, D. and Chen, K.-H. (eds) *Stuart Hall: critical dialogues in cultural studies*, London, Routledge.

HALL, S. with CRUZ, J. and LEWIS, J. (eds) (1994) 'Reflections of the encoding/decoding model: an interview with Stuart Hall' in Cruz, J. and Lewis, J. (eds).

HALL, S. (ed.) (1997) *Representation: cultural representations and signifying practices*, London, Sage/The Open University (Book 2 in this series).

HARVEY, T. A. (1988) 'How Sony Corp. became first with kids', *AdWeek's Marketing Week,* 21 November, pp. 58–9.

HEBDIGE, D. (1979) *Subculture: the meaning of style,* London, Methuen.

HORKHEIMER, M. and ADORNO, T. W. (1979) *Dialectic of Enlightenment* London, Verso (first pub. 1947).

HOSOKAWA, S. (1984) 'The Walkman effect', *Popular Music*, Vol. 4, pp. 165–80.

JACKSON, V. (1994) 'Menace II Society', *Touch*, No. 42, November, pp. 15–17.

JAPANESE INDUSTRIAL DESIGN ASSOCIATION (1983) *Structure of Dexterity: industrial design works in Japan*, Rikuyo-Sha, Japan.

JOHNSON, R. (1986) 'The story so far: and for the transformations' in Punter, D. (ed.) *Introduction to Contemporary Cultural Studies*, London, Longman, pp. 277–313.

KLEIN, L. (1979) 'Audio update', *Radio Electronics*.

KNIGHT, J. (1992) 'Walkman inventor is knighted', *The Times*, 5 October.

KUROKI, Y. (1987) *Walkman Style Planning Technique*.

LEE, O.-YOUNG (1982) *The Compact Culture: the Japanese tradition of 'Smaller is Better'*, Japan, Kodansha International.

LYONS, N. (1976) *The Sony Vision*, New York, Crown Publishers Inc.

MACKAY, H. (ed.) (1997) *Consumption and Everyday Life*, London, Sage/The Open University (Book 5 in this series).

MARCUSE, H. (1964) *One Dimensional Man,* London, Routledge.

MARX, K. (1980) *Marx's Grundrisse*, selected and edited by David McLellan, London, Paladin (written 1857–8).

MASSEY, D. (1991) 'A global sense of place', *Marxism Today*, June.

MILLER, C. (1992) 'Sony's product "playground" yields insight on consumer behaviour', *Marketing News*, 3 February, pp. 2, 13.

MILLER, D. (1987) *Material Culture and Mass Consumption*, Oxford, Blackwell.

MILLS, C. W. (1951) *White Collar*, Oxford, Oxford University Press.

MORITA, A., REINGOLD, E. and SHIMOMURE, M. (1987) *Made in Japan: Akio Morita and Sony*, London, Collins.

MORLEY, D. (1992) *Television, Audiences and Cultural Studies,* London, Routledge.

MORLEY, D. (1994) 'Between the public and the private: the domestic uses of information and communications technologies' in Cruz, J. and Lewis, J. (eds).

MORLEY, D. and ROBINS, K. (1992) 'Techno-Orientalism: foreigners, phobias and futures', *New Formations: a journal of culture/theory/politics*, No. 16, pp. 136–56.

NAKAMOTO, M. (1994) 'Morita resigns as Chairman of Sony', *Financial Times*, 26 November, p. 13.

NARAYAN, N. and KATZ, I. (1993) 'Judgement is music to Sony's ears', *The Guardian*, 14 January, p. 22.

NEGUS, K. (1992) *Producing Pop*, London, Edward Arnold.

NEGUS, K. (1997) 'The production of culture' in du Gay, P. (ed.).

NEW YORKER, THE (1989) 'Walkman (Listening to Music in NYC)', 2 January, pp. 19–20.

NOLL, M. (1987) 'The Walkman cometh', *Christianity Today*, 6 February, pp. 22–3.

PIORE, M. J. and SABEL, C. (1984) *The Second Industrial Divide: prospects for prosperity*, New York, Basic Books.

PRATT, M. L (1992) *Imperial Eyes: studies in travel-writing and transculturation*, London, Routledge.

RAFFERTY, K. and BANNISTER, N. (1994) 'Mr Walkman steps down', *The Guardian*, 26 November, p. 38.

ROBINS, K. (1991) 'Tradition and translation: national culture in its global context' in Corner, J. and Harvey, S. (eds) *Enterprise and Heritage: crosscurrents of national culture*, London, Routledge.

SANGER, D. (1990) 'Sony's Norio Ohga: building smaller, buying bigger', *New York Times Magazine*.

SCHAFER, R. M. (1977) *The Tuning of the World*, New York, Knopf.

SCHLENDER, B. (1992) 'How Sony keeps the magic going', *Fortune*, 24 February, pp. 22–7.

SONY (1989) *The Case of the Walkman*, Sony's Innovations in Management Series, Vol. 1, Corporate Communications, Sony Corporation.

SPARKE, P. (1986) *An Introduction to Design and Culture in the Twentieth Century*, London, Allen and Unwin.

SPARKE, P. (1987) *Japanese Design*, London, Michael Joseph.

SPICE, N. (1995) 'Hubbub', *The London Review of Books*, 6 July, pp. 3–6.

STEARNS, R. (1981) 'Personal portable stereo units are selling out faster than manufacturers can meet demand', *Merchandising*, September, pp. 90–91.

TAYLOR, S. (1988) 'The other side of Sony', *Arena*, Spring, pp. 123–7.

THOMPSON, K. (ed.) (1997) *Media and Cultural Regulation*, London, Sage/The Open University (Book 6 in this series).

TOBIN, J. J. (ed.) (1992) *Re-made in Japan: everyday life and consumer taste in a changing society*, Newhaven, CT, and London, Yale University Press.

UEYAMA, S. (1982) 'The selling of the Walkman', *Advertising Age*, 22 March.

VEBLEN, T. (1957) *The Theory of the Leisure Class*, London, George Allen and Unwin (first pub. 1899).

WALLIN, N. (1986) 'The modern soundscape and noise pollution', *The Courier (UNESCO)*, April, pp. 31–3.

WEBER, M. (1950) *The Methodology of the Social Sciences*, New York, The Free Press (essays written 1903–07).

WILLIAMS, R. (1961) *The Long Revolution*, Penguin, Harmondsworth.

WILLIAMS, R. (1976) *Keywords*, London, Fontana.

WILLIAMS, R. (1983) *Towards 2000*, London, Chatto & Windus/The Hogarth Press.

WILLIAMSON, J. (1986) 'The problems of being popular', *New Socialist*, 41, pp. 14–15.

WILLIS, P. (1978) *Profane Culture,* London, Routledge and Kegan Paul.

WOODWARD, K. (ed.) (1997) *Identity and Difference*, London, Sage/The Open University (Book 3 in this series).

READING A
Walter Benjamin : 'The work of art in the age of mechanical reproduction'

I

In principle a work of art has always been reproducible. Man-made artefacts could always be imitated by men. Replicas were made by pupils in practice of their craft, by masters for diffusing their works, and, finally, by third parties in the pursuit of gain. Mechanical reproduction of a work of art, however, represents something new. Historically, it advanced intermittently and in leaps at long intervals, but with accelerated intensity. The Greeks knew only two procedures of technically reproducing works of art: founding and stamping. Bronzes, terra cottas, and coins were the only art works which they could produce in quantity. All others were unique and could not be mechanically reproduced. With the woodcut graphic art became mechanically reproducible for the first time, long before script became reproducible by print. The enormous changes which printing, the mechanical reproduction of writing, has brought about in literature are a familiar story. However, within the phenomenon which we are here examining from the perspective of world history, print is merely a special, though particularly important, case. During the Middle Ages engraving and etching were added to the woodcut; at the beginning of the nineteenth century lithography made its appearance.

With lithography the technique of reproduction reached an essentially new stage. This much more direct process was distinguished by the tracing of the design on a stone rather than its incision on a block of wood or its etching on a copperplate and permitted graphic art for the first time to put its products on the market, not only in large numbers as hitherto, but also in daily changing forms. Lithography enabled graphic art to illustrate everyday life, and it began to keep pace with printing. But only a few decades after its invention, lithography was surpassed by photography. For the first time in the process of pictorial reproduction, photography freed the hand of the most important artistic functions which henceforth devolved only upon the eye looking into a lens. Since the eye perceives more swiftly than the hand can draw, the

process of pictorial reproduction was accelerated so enormously that it could keep pace with speech. A film operator shooting a scene in the studio captures the images at the speed of an actor's speech. Just as lithography virtually implied the illustrated newspaper, so did photography foreshadow the sound film. The technical reproduction of sound was tackled at the end of the last century. These convergent endeavors made predictable a situation which Paul Valéry pointed up in this sentence: 'Just as water, gas, and electricity are brought into our houses from far off to satisfy our needs in response to a minimal effort, so we shall be supplied with visual or auditory images, which will appear and disappear at a simple movement of the hand, hardly more than a sign' (1964, p. 226). Around 1900 technical reproduction had reached a standard that not only permitted it to reproduce all transmitted works of art and thus to cause the most profound change in their impact upon the public; it also had captured a place of its own among the artistic processes. For the study of this standard nothing is more revealing than the nature of the repercussions that these two different manifestations – the reproduction of works of art and the art of the film – have had on art in its traditional form.

II

Even the most perfect reproduction of a work of art is lacking in one element: its presence in time and space, its unique existence at the place where it happens to be. This unique existence of the work of art determined the history to which it was subject throughout the time of its existence. [...]

The presence of the original is the prerequisite to the concept of authenticity. Chemical analyses of the patina of a bronze can help to establish this, as does the proof that a given manuscript of the Middle Age stems from an archive of the fifteenth century. The whole sphere of authenticity is outside technical – and, of course, not only technical – reproducibility. Confronted with its manual reproduction, which was usually branded as a forgery, the original preserved all its authority; not so vis-à-vis technical reproduction. The reason is twofold. First, [mechanical] reproduction is more independent of the original than manual reproduction. For example, in photography, reproduction can bring out those aspects of the original that are unattainable to the naked eye yet accessible to the lens, which is adjustable and chooses its angle at will. And photographic reproduction, with the aid of certain processes, such as enlargement or slow motion, can capture images which escape natural vision. Secondly, technical reproduction can put the copy of the original into situations which would be out of reach for the original itself. Above all, it enables the original to meet the beholder halfway, be it in the form of a photograph or a phonograph record. The cathedral leaves its locale to be received in the studio of a lover of art; the choral production, performed in an auditorium or in the open air, resounds in the drawing room.

The situations into which the product of mechanical reproduction can be brought may not touch the actual work of art, yet the quality of its presence is always depreciated. This holds not only for the art work but also, for instance, for a landscape which passes in review before the spectator in a movie. In the case of the art object, a most sensitive nucleus – namely, its authenticity – is interfered with whereas no natural object is vulnerable on that score. [...]

One might subsume the eliminated element in the term 'aura' and go on to say: that which withers in the age of mechanical reproduction is the aura of the work of art. This is a symptomatic process whose significance points beyond the realm of art. One might generalize by saying: the technique of reproduction detaches the reproduced object from the domain of tradition. By making many reproductions it substitutes a plurality of copies for a unique existence. And in permitting the reproduction to meet the beholder or listener in his own particular situation, it reactivates the object reproduced. These two processes lead to a tremendous shattering of tradition which is the obverse of the contemporary crisis and renewal of mankind. Both processes are intimately connected with the contemporary mass movements. Their most powerful agent is the film. Its social significance, particularly in its most positive form, is inconceivable without its destructive, cathartic aspect, that is, the liquidation of the traditional value of the cultural heritage. This phenomenon is most palpable in the great historical films. It extends to ever new positions. In 1927 Abel Gance exclaimed enthusiastically: 'Shakespeare, Rembrandt, Beethoven will make films...all legends, all mythologies and all myths, all founders of religion, and the very religions... await their

exposed resurrection, and the heroes crowd each other at the gate' [Gance, 1927]. Presumably without intending it, he issued an invitation to a far-reaching liquidation.

III

During long periods of history, the mode of human sense perception changes with humanity's entire mode of existence. The manner in which human sense perception is organized, the medium in which it is accomplished, is determined not only by nature but by historical circumstances as well. [...]

The concept of aura which was proposed above with reference to historical objects may usefully be illustrated with reference to the aura of natural ones. We define the aura of the latter as the unique phenomenon of a distance, however close it may be. If, while resting on a summer afternoon, you follow with your eyes a mountain range on the horizon or a branch which casts its shadow over you, you experience the aura of those mountains, of that branch. This image makes it easy to comprehend the social bases of the contemporary decay of the aura. It rests on two circumstances, both of which are related to the increasing significance of the masses in contemporary life. Namely, the desire of the contemporary masses to bring things 'closer' spatially and humanly, which is just as ardent as their bent toward overcoming the uniqueness of every reality by accepting its reproduction. Every day the urge grows stronger to get hold of an object at very close range by way of its likeness, its reproduction. Unmistakably, reproduction as offered by picture magazines and newsreels differs from the image seen by the unarmed eye. Uniqueness and permanence are as closely linked in the latter as are transitoriness and reproducibility in the former. To pry an object from its shell, to destroy its aura, is the mark of a perception whose 'sense of the universal equality of things' has increased to such a degree that it extracts it even from a unique object by means of reproduction. Thus is manifested in the field of perception what in the theoretical sphere is noticeable in the increasing importance of statistics. The adjustment of reality to the masses and of the masses to reality is a process of unlimited scope, as much for thinking as for perception.

IV

The uniqueness of a work of art is inseparable from its being imbedded in the fabric of tradition. This tradition itself is thoroughly alive and extremely changeable. An ancient statue of Venus, for example, stood in a different traditional context with the Greeks, who made it an object of veneration, than with the clerics of the Middle Ages, who viewed it as an ominous idol. Both of them, however, were equally confronted with its uniqueness, that is, its aura. Originally the contextual integration of art in tradition found its expression in the cult. We know that the earliest art works originated in the service of a ritual – first the magical, then the religious kind. It is significant that the existence of the work of art with reference to its aura is never entirely separated from its ritual function. In other words, the unique vale of the 'authentic' work of art has its basis in ritual, the location of its original use value. This ritualistic basis, however remote, is still recognizable as secularized ritual even in the most profane forms of the cult of beauty. The secular cult of beauty, developed during the Renaissance and prevailing for three centuries, clearly showed that ritualistic basis in its decline and the first deep crisis which befell it. With the advent of the first truly revolutionary means of reproduction, photography, simultaneously with the rise of socialism, art sensed the approaching crisis which has become evident a century later. At the time, art reacted with the doctrine of *l'art pour l'art*, that is, with a theology of art. This gave rise to what might be called a negative theology in the form of the idea of 'pure' art, which not only denied any social function of art but also any categorizing by subject matter. (In poetry, Mallarmé was the first to take this position.)

An analysis of art in the age of mechanical reproduction must do justice to these relationships, for they lead us to an all-important insight: for the first time in world history, mechanical reproduction emancipates the work of art from its parasitical dependence on ritual. To an ever greater degree the work of art reproduced becomes the work of art designed for reproducibility. From a photographic negative, for example, one can make any number of prints; to ask for the 'authentic' print makes no sense. But the instant the criterion of authenticity ceases to be applicable to artistic production, the total function of art is reversed. Instead of being based on ritual, it begins to be based on another practice – politics.

V

Works of art are received and valued on different planes. Two polar types stand out: with one, the accent is on the cult value; with the other, on the exhibition value of the work. Artistic production begins with ceremonial objects destined to serve in a cult. One may assume that what mattered was their existence, not their being on view. The elk portrayed by the man of the Stone Age on the walls of his cave was an instrument of magic. He did expose it to his fellow men, but in the main it was meant for the spirits. Today the cult value would seem to demand that the work of art remain hidden. Certain statues of gods are accessible only to the priest in the cella; certain Madonnas remain covered nearly all year round; certain sculptures on medieval cathedrals are invisible to the spectator on ground level. With the emancipation of the various art practices from ritual go increasing opportunities for the exhibition of their products. It is easier to exhibit a portrait bust that can be sent here and there than to exhibit the statue of a divinity that has its fixed place in the interior of a temple. The same holds for the painting as against the mosaic or fresco that preceded it. And even though the public presentability of a mass originally may have been just as great as that of a symphony, the latter originated at the moment when its public presentability promised to surpass that of the mass.

With the different methods of technical reproduction of a work of art, its fitness for exhibition increased to such an extent that the quantitative shift between its two poles turned into a qualitative transformation of its nature. This is comparable to the situation of the work of art in prehistoric times when, by the absolute emphasis on its cult value, it was, first and foremost, an instrument of magic. Only later did it come to be recognised as a work of art. In the same way today, by the absolute emphasis on its exhibition value the work of art becomes a creation with entirely new functions, among which the one we are conscious of, the artistic function, later may be recognised as incidental. This much is certain: today photography and the film are the most serviceable exemplifications of this new function.

References

GANCE, A. (1927) 'Le Temps de l'image est venu', *L'Art Cinématographique*, Vol. 2, pp. 94f, Paris.

VALÉRY, P. (1964) 'The conquest of ubiquity' in *Aesthetics*, trans. by Ralph Mannheim, New York, Pantheon Books Bollingen Series.

Source: Benjamin, 1970, pp. 220–7.

READING B
Raymond Williams: 'Mobile privatization'

Most human beings adjust, because they must, to altered, even radically altered conditions. This is already marked in the first generations of such shifts. By the second and third generations the initially enforced conditions are likely to have become if not the new social norms – for at many levels of intensity the conditions may still be resented – *at least the new social perspective, its everyday common sense*. Moreover, because so many of the shifts are enforced by a willed exploitation of new means of production and new products, sometimes ending in failure but much more often increasing goods of every kind, there are major if always unequal material advantages in the new conditions. Capitalism as a system, just because of its inherent one-dimensional mobility, can move on very rapidly from its failures and worked-out areas, leaving only local peoples stuck with them. By its very single-mindedness it can direct new and advantageous production in at least the short-term interests of effective working majorities. In any of its periodic crises it can make from one in ten to one in three of a numbered people redundant, but while it still has the other nine or the other two it can usually gain sufficient support or tolerance to continue its operations. Moreover, identified almost inextricably with positive advantages in improved products and services, it not only claims but is acclaimed as progress.

Thus while on an historical or comparative scale its forced operations are bound to be seen as arbitrary and often brutal, on any local and temporarily settled scale it flies with the wings of the dove. It brings factories and supermarkets, employment and affluence, and everything else is a local and temporary difficulty – out of sight, out of time, out of mind – or is the evident fault, even the malign fault, of those who are suffering. In any general examination, the system is transparent, and ugly. But in many, and so far always enough, local perspectives it is not only the tolerated but the consciously preferred order of real majorities.

For now from the other side of its mouth it speaks of the consumer: the satisfied, even stuffed consumer; the sovereign consumer. Sovereign? That raises a problem, but while the production lines flow and the shopping trolleys are ready to carry the goods away, there is this new, powerful social identity, which is readily and even eagerly adopted. It is at best a radically reduced identity, at worst mean and greedy. But of course 'consumer' is only a general purpose word, on the lines of 'citizen' or 'subject'. It is accepted only as describing that level of life: the bustling level of the supermarket. When the goods from the trolley have been stowed in the car, and the car is back home, a fuller and more human identity is ready at the turn of a key: a family, a marriage, children, relatives, friends. The economic behaviour of the consumer is something you move out to, so as to bring the good things back.

There is then a unique modern condition, which I defined in an earlier book (*Television: technology and cultural form*, 1974) as 'mobile privatisation'. It is an ugly phrase for an unprecedented condition. What it means is that at most active social levels people are increasingly living as private small-family units, or, disrupting even that, as private and deliberately self-enclosed individuals, while at the same time there is a quite unprecedented mobility of such restricted privacies. In my novel *Second Generation* (1964) I developed the image of modern car traffic to describe this now dominant set of social relations in the old industrial societies. Looked at from right outside, the traffic flows and their regulation are clearly a social order of a determined kind, yet what is experienced inside them – in the conditioned atmosphere and internal music of this windowed shell – is movement, choice of direction, the pursuit of self-determined private purposes. All the other shells are moving, in comparable ways but for their own different private ends. They are not so much other people, in any full sense, but other units which signal and are signalled to, so that private mobilities can proceed safely and relatively unhindered. And if all this is seen from outside as in deep ways determined, or in some sweeping glance as dehumanised, that is not at all how it feels like inside the shell, with people you want to be with, going where you want to go.

Thus at a now dominant level of social relations, systems quite other than settlement, or in any of its older senses community, are both active and continually reproduced. The only disturbance is when movements from quite outside them – movements which are the real workings of the

effective but taken-for-granted public system – slow the flow, change the prices, depreciate or disrupt the employee–consumer connection: forcing a truly public world back into a chosen and intensely valued privacy.

The international market in every kind of commodity receives its deep assent from this system of mobile-privatised social relations. From the shell, whether house or car or employment, the only relevant calculations are the terms of continuing or improving its own conditions. If buying what such calculations indicate, from another dominated nominal 'nation', leads directly or indirectly to the breaking or weakening of other people's shells, 'too bad' do we say? But the connections are not often as direct as that. They work their way through an immensely complicated and often unreadable market system. The results emerge as statistics, or as general remarks in television. Mainly what is wrong, we usually conclude, is what all those other shells are doing.

References

WILLIAMS, R. (1974) *Television: technology and cultural form*, London, Fontana.

WILLIAMS, R. (1964) *Second Generation*, London, Chatto & Windus.

Source: Williams, 1983, pp. 187–9.

READING C
Nick Lyons: 'Scratching a global dream'

When Morita came to the United States for the first time in 1953, primarily to sign the contract with Western Electric, he received two shocks: American industry was positively awesome and the general American consumer still read the phrase 'Made in Japan' as infallible proof of cheapness.

'As early as the 1870s,' suggests Noel F. Busch, 'most Japanese traders had concluded that their opposite numbers from the United States and Europe were in most cases tasteless bargain hunters interested in the cheapest merchandise available.' So they made, chiefly for export, 'Yokohama *muke*', which flooded the markets with jerry-built junk that became synonymous with Japanese products. Only in 1950, when such prominent photographers as Carl Mydans and Alfred Eisenstadt replaced their German Leicas with Japanese Nikons, did the West have a glimmer of Japanese technological skill. 'The camera manufacturers,' says Morita, 'did us an invaluable service'. But photography was a limited field – and what the best photographers knew of and used was not what the masses bought. It would take another decade or more for the association of Japan and junk to fade.

The United States, when Morita landed in San Francisco, seemed so huge, so advanced. 'How can we compete with these people?' he wondered. He admits frankly that his first reaction was one of utter dejection: he felt defeated by the size and scale of American industry. It would be impossible to compete here, to sell his products in a country with such advanced technology, with such large, smoothly functioning companies.

After he had signed with Western Electric he flew to Germany; he was not more encouraged. Germany, too, had been destroyed in the war, but was already highly advanced. He visited Volkswagen, Mercedes-Benz, Telefunken, and other major firms – able to speak none of the European languages, bumbling and shy at first with his textbook high-school English. He saw virtually no other Japanese. English was the only foreign language he could manage at all, and he soon found himself relying on it more and more. 'It was the only way to communicate,' he recalls. 'I knew it was the international language and that I would have to learn it.' He carried a dictionary through Germany, France, and Switzerland, alone and often lonely or lost, making friends with an American who was also lost, finally growing bold with his English, recognizing that only when he lost all hesitation could he make the language the working tool it must become for him.

What he saw of European industry confirmed his feeling of defeat: he 'lost all fight,' he says; he could not possibly compete in this market either.

Only three years earlier, Edwin O. Reischauer had said: 'The economic situation in Japan may be fundamentally so unsound that no policies, no matter how wise, can save her from slow economic starvation.' Not only had the country been devastated but it was one of the poorest in natural resources in the world – needing to import more than 99 per cent of all its crude oil, cotton and wool, and iron ore.

But despite the most dour predictions of wise observers, Japanese industry – and Morita's small company – had begun to grow. Steadily, through the marshalling of all its forces in what amounted to a national campaign, the little resource-poor country, defeated psychologically as well as physically by the war, was commencing what in less than ten years would be called 'the economic miracle of Japan, Inc.'.

Source: Lyons, 1976, pp. 56–9.

READING D
Shu Ueyama: 'The selling of the "Walkman"'

Birth of the Walkman

As with many other great inventions, the birth of the Walkman was accidental.

In October, 1978, there was an organizational change in Sony's audio division. The tape recorder division, which had been producing radio-cassette recorders and tape recorders, was told that it would not be making the former any longer; this product category was transferred to the radio division.

So the tape recorder division was in trouble. It had to generate new business to sustain the same profitability as before. The staff got together and had serious discussions day and night for a week. Then came a brilliant idea: to make a portable stereo recorder.

At that time, Sony had two compact type recorders: one was a semiprofessional monaural recorder called the 'Pressman'; the other was a dictating machine for business usage. Because the latter already had double-track recording and playback facility, it was not too difficult to convert it into a normal four-track stereo recorder.

Sony staff members connected this recorder to a pair of large and heavy headphones. The sound quality was superb. The engineers who made this prototype still recollect the excitement they experienced when they heard the sound for the first time.

This clumsy looking machine hooked to a pair of clumsy headphones was the beginning of the Walkman.

Another accident followed several days later. Masaru Ibuka, honorary chairman and co-founder of Sony, causally dropped in on the tape-recorder division and saw this strange looking prototype.

He listened to it and thought it could be an interesting product. But he thought the headphones were too big and heavy.

Because he knew that the research laboratory was experimenting with new lightweight headphones at that time, he recommended the two be combined.

Akio Morita, Sony's chairman, heard about this prototype from Mr Ibuka and asked the engineers to bring the machine to his office. He felt the same excitement he experienced when he first introduced transistor radios.

Mr Morita borrowed the set during the following weekend. He went to play golf with his friends and took it with him. He and one of his golfing friends listened to the recorder because the machine already had two headphone plug-ins. But they found it rather inconvenient not to be able to converse with each other with their headphones on.

On Monday, he proposed to the engineers that a special switch be added to suppress the volume of music momentarily when one wishes to have a conversation. It was later named 'the hot-line switch'.

The engineers incorporated this idea and several others, and they completed the final design and specifications on March 24, 1979, five months after the tape recorder division lost its radio-cassette business.

The Walkman Team

When Mr Morita saw a tremendous potential in this new product, he gathered 10 people from different Sony divisions: production, product planning, design, advertising, sales and export. They became the members of the 'Walkman Team', a group set up to decide all the strategies for the Walkman. Mr Morita appointed himself project manager.

Such a team approach was necessary to launch the Walkman within six months. It usually takes one or two years to make a new product.

At meetings, the team discussed specifications of the new model. The production schedule was drawn, and a decision was made on the quantity to be produced. Cost structure and pricing were also decided. There were heated discussion about what to name the product. Various promotional ideas were formulated. Package designs were presented. Presale consumer tests were conducted. All the conceivable activities surrounding the Walkman business were discussed thoroughly in this group.

Marketing the Walkman

The first prototype was made by converting a set of the Pressman, which retailed at 42,800 yen ($186). Stereo circuitry, a stereo playback head and a pair of headphones were added, but the speaker was eliminated. Then, a cost estimate helped establish a price of $217. This was presented at a Walkman Team meeting.

Mr Morita thought it was too expensive. The customer profile of the Pressman was primarily professional reporters and writers who could afford such a high price. Because he had teenagers in his mind as the target customers for the Walkman, he thought it would be necessary to bring down the price drastically, to around the level of $130.

The price of any mass-produced consumer good goes down as production quantity increases. So, even if a product is showing a deficit in its initial production lot, the production cost lowers when it is produced in the millions.

The cost reduction curve depends totally on the cumulative production quantity. If the cost of a plastic mold or a die is amortized by millions then the cost distributed to each unit becomes minimal. But the problem was that nobody was quite sure how many Walkmans could be sold. No one, except possibly Mr Morita, thought they would eventually become such a sensational best seller all over the world.

Mr Morita, with a mischievous smile on his face, suggested the selling price of 33,000 yen ($143). He explained the reason to the members of the Walkman Team: "Well, gentlemen, this year we happen to be celebrating the 33rd anniversary of our company."

At this price, the tape recorder division would be losing money in the beginning, however, hard it tried to bring down the production cost. But Mr Morita was convinced the Walkman would eventually make money.

The production started. The factory tried its best to bring down its production costs in each stage. The fact that all the key parts, such as motors, stereo heads and headphones, were being produced within the Sony operation eliminated unnecessary negotiations of price reduction.

Each division shed a little blood and cooperated with the corporate decision.

Normally, circuitry and mechanical engineers do not get involved in production after they have finished their assignments of designing the product. But in the case of the Walkman, they were deeply involved in its production because of the cost reduction they had to achieve.

Changes in circuitry design were made by incorporating ICs (Integrated Circuitries) instead of normal transistors and resistors, thus bringing down the number of parts and the cost. These efforts and the increase of production gradually brought down the production cost, and the Walkman became more profitable each month.

Source: Ueyama, 1982.

READING E
Thomas A. Harvey: 'How Sony Corporation became first with kids'

Brand loyalty at a young age

After the first meeting the concept idea heated up very quickly. We got the design centre and advertising people involved. A product planning cycle that would usually take Sony fourteen months was harnessed to launch My First Sony in less than one year.

Once we had the name My First Sony we asked ourselves: why should we send a message to a child that Sony manufactures cheap radios? If we could create a product that made a long-term, favourable impression on children and be comparable in quality with the rest of the Sony line Americans know so well, we'd be building brand loyalty at a young age.

The target audience

Our target market is adults, generally working couples who are reasonably affluent. Sony is a brand name parents recognize and it connotes a quality image to them. Purchasers of children's products divide into two groups, those who are brand conscious and those who are price conscious. If parents are price conscious, they'll buy an inexpensive toy for their child and if it breaks in two months they'll throw it away. But price sensitivity wasn't our biggest concern – product quality was. If we put out a product that didn't work well, we'd lose a lot of adult confidence that we'd spent years building up.

Saving for the kids

In focus groups, parents agreed with our premise that there was a niche for quality electronics for kids. But they were sceptical about pricing – most of the products range from $34.95 to $89.95. The CD player introduced this year costs $199.

But quite frankly, even if parents had told us the idea was terrible, we'd still have gone ahead with it. Years ago, when Sony first showed the Walkman to dealers here in the US, they thought the company was crazy trying to sell a $200 stereo that didn't even record. But the company has a long history of pushing through products it believes in. Besides, there's a lot more marketing of upscale products to young consumers today. Parents who religiously scrimp and save on items for themselves will often have no trouble spending that extra dollar on something for their children.

Shopping trips

The first thing we did when we started designing the product was to visit toy stores and buy as many electronic toys as we could find. Many manufacturers simply take a well-known character like Mickey Mouse and put his picture on a tape recorder. We wanted My First Sony to look more like electronics products that already existed in the adult market, with special adaptations for kids. For instance, the radios and tape recorders for children had to be more durable and the corners rounded so they weren't sharp.

We also noticed during our store visits that toys for boys tended to be orange and black and toys for girls were pink and purple. We wanted something that would appeal to both sexes and age levels from four to eleven. So we decided to go for bright primary colours with universal appeal for children – red, blue, green and yellow.

A see-through package

The design team also spent several days in toy stores watching parents buying toys for their children. That led to an important decision about our packaging. We noticed that even though there were signs saying 'Don't Open the Packages' parents always ripped the boxes apart. Parents really wanted to hold and touch the product. So we used a see-through window on the front of the box that allows them to see the entire product without having to touch it.

Mother knows best

When children's products in toy stores and department stores are produced below $100, mothers make over sixty per cent of the purchasing decisions. Once you reach $100, the fathers start getting involved. Children have direct involvement in purchasing when the parent is buying something like an action figure or a GI Joe doll, but not with a product perceived as educational. So we advertise on national television to reach both parents, but avoid Saturday morning cartoon shows which only kids watch. We also run print ads in women's magazines.

The advertising strategy

We spent about $2-to-$3 million to build awareness for the line. Your average toy commercial is a real flight of fancy for the child. Our commercials are aimed at parents. We asked our ad agencies to come up with spots that would assail mom's emotions rather than her mind. We wanted embraceable kids from a cross-section of America rather than highly stylized, up-scale children. The agencies came up with two variations of the song 'I like pizza pie, I like macaroni, but what I love is My First Sony'. Print ads show a group of children holding and playing with our products.

The retail environment

My First Sony has created a new merchandise category for toy stores and also helped attract a more affluent customer. We started out selling My First Sony to up-scale department stores and toy stores like Toys'R'Us and Child's World. Toy stores are the best vehicles for us. They attract customer traffic on a regular basis and kids drag their parents to them on the weekends. Now we're also expanding into some key electronics-retailers like Circuit City and selling in Europe and Japan.

Not a toy company

Sony does not want to be in the toy business, because it's very competitive and price sensitive. Once someone comes up with a new idea for a toy, another manufacturer will knock it off and steal market share like crazy. We're competing for shelf space with a lot of toy manufacturers, but we see the toy market as very different than ours. My First Sony is an electronics line for children. Adult electronics is gimmicky – we're pre-conditioned to look every year for a new model of the product we own. But with children, as long as the product meets their demands, they won't need another one for four or five years.

Expanding the line

This year we introduced five new products. These include the first CD player for children, a cassette tape-recorder and a wrist walkie-talkie. Our original products were versions of our adult products for kids. The second generation products are more sophisticated and offer interactive capabilities. They present much more of a learning experience for the child. For instance, the new cassette-recorder allows children to sing along with their favourite music and record their own voices. In the future, we may move into higher-end educational electronics product for children.

Music and software promotions

There is a lot of children's music and educational software available to parents but many are not aware of how much is actually out there. This fall we decided to team up with music companies to jointly increase our sales.

We launched a joint promotion with A&M Records, for example, this fall. It is a sampling program designed to help build awareness of compact discs for children. A CD of children's recordings is packaged inside about 10,000 My First Sony CD player boxes. We also launched a promotion this September with Peter Pan Industries. Consumers who purchase any of the My First Sony tape players will also receive two free sing-along cassettes.

Source: Harvey, 1988, pp. 58–9.

READING F
Rey Chow: 'Listening otherwise, music miniaturized: a different type of question about revolution'

The collective and the composite

Any attempt to construct a discourse about contemporary Chinese popular music needs to come to terms with the fact that many linguistically determined senses of 'discourse' do not work. One can even say that much of this music is about the inability or the refusal to articulate and to talk. This is not simply because humans are, after all, animals that cannot be defined by their speech alone. It is also because inarticulateness is a way of combating the talking function of the state, the most *articulate* organ that speaks for everyone.

When you listen to the songs by mainland China's young singers such as Cui Jian, you'll find that they are lively, Westernized, and full of the kind of physical, rhythmic quality that we associate with rock music. Cui Jian's music poses a familiar problem about the emotions involved in our listening – the problem of physicality. Adorno has warned us against such physicality: 'The physical aspect of music ... is not indicative of a natural state – of an essence pure and free of all ideology – but rather it accords with the retrogression of society.' The diatribe of retrogression is a formidable heirloom in the house of popular cultural theories. But treasures of the past are most valuable when they are pawned for more pressing needs of the present. If the physicality of a particular music is indeed retrogressive, we need to ask why.

Contemporary popular Chinese music raises many issues similar to those of rock-and-roll in the West. Foremost among these is that of the music's critical function in regard to the dominant culture. Any consideration of popular cultural forms confronts questions like the following: if such forms provide alternative practical consciousness to the dominant ideology, are the modes of subversion and resistance in them not infinitely reabsorbed by the dominant culture? Are such forms capable of maintaining their autonomy? Furthermore, how do we come to grips with such practical consciousness when that category indispensable to traditional Marxist social analysis – class – seems no longer adequate in mapping the cultural differentiations that persist beyond class distinctions? Take the example of American popular music. For many critics, the problem posed by this music is how to locate in it a genuinely oppositional function when class distinctions in the United States are more often elided than clearly defined. One might say that it is the impossibility of identifying any distinct class struggle – and with that, the impossibility of legitimizing the notion of class struggle itself for social criticism – that in part accounts for Adorno's reading of American popular music as a massive numbing. The blurring of class distinctions – as reflected in 'easy listening' music – is inordinately discomforting for the sober Frankfurt School critic.

It is, thus, when we focus on what still remains for many as an indispensable category in social criticism – class struggle – that contemporary Chinese popular music, despite its resonances with Western popular music, poses the greatest enigma. China is a 'Third World' nation, and yet where do we find the expression of class struggle in its popular cultural forms these days? Instead of exhibiting the classic 'symptom' of a 'Third World' nation in the form of an obsession with 'class', contemporary Chinese popular culture 'speaks' a different language of 'oppressed' emotions. In the realm of music, we find the conscious adoption of Western models of rhythm, instrumentality, recording, and modes of distribution for the production of discourses which are *non-Western in the sense of an inattentiveness to class struggle*. Many of the motifs that surface in contemporary Chinese popular music, like their counterparts in fiction, television, and film, can be described as individualist and populist – troublesome terms for Western Marxists who at one point looked to Communist China for its utopian aspirations. Such motifs are surfacing at a time when the mainland Chinese official ideology is still firmly 'communist'. Therefore, while the perception of class is undoubtedly present in the subversive emotions of contemporary Chinese popular music, it is present less as an agency for struggle than as the disciplinary cliché of the dominant culture *to be struggled against*. This is precisely because 'class struggle' has been lived through not merely in the form of critical talk but also in everyday experience, as official ideology and national culture. (In mainland China, 'struggle' is a transitive verb, an act one performs directly on another: thus, 'to struggle someone'.)

Speaking of his inability to deal with the directly political, Roland Barthes says (in an interview): 'these days a discourse that is not impassioned can't be heard, quite simply. There's a decibel threshold that must be crossed for discourse to be heard.' Barthes's statement offers us a way of defining 'dominant' culture in musical terms, not only as that which crosses a particular decibel threshold as a rule, but also as that which collectivizes and mobilizes with its particular loud, indeed deafening, decibel level. If revolution is, among other things, a technology of sound, then its mode of implementation is that of mechanized and institutionalized recording, repetition, and simplification. As early as 1928, the Chinese writer and critic Mao Dun used the technology of sound in a discussion of 'proletarian literature' to indicate the danger of the new political orthodoxy which based its moves on prescriptive slogans: 'I ... cannot believe that making oneself into a gramophone shouting "This is the way out, come this way!" has any value or can leave one with an easy conscience. It is precisely because I do not wish to stifle my conscience and say things I do not believe ... that I cannot make the characters in my novelette [*Pursuit*] find a way out.'

The past forty years of Chinese communism can be described as a history in which class struggle is used as the foundation for the official culture of a nation state [...] Entwined with nationalism and patriotism, and strategically deployed by the state, 'the people's speech' that supposedly results from successful class struggle forms the cadences of sonorous music. One thinks of pieces such as the 'International Song', 'Dongfanghong' (The east is red), 'Meiyou gongchandang meiyou xin zhongguo' (There would be no new China without the Communist Party), and many others that are standardized for official celebrations to invoke patriotic sentiments. Official state culture champions an irresistible grid of emotions that can be defined by Susan Stewart's notion of 'the gigantic', which 'we find ... at the origin of public and natural history' (Stewart, 1984, p. 71). Gigantic emotions are the emotions of reverence, dedication, discipline, and nostalgia, all of which have to do with the preservation of history as it ought to be remembered. In a Third World nation whose history is characterized by a struggle against imperialism as well as internal turmoil, the history that 'ought to be remembered' is the history of the successful collectivization of the people for the establishment of a national community.

Many examples of contemporary Chinese popular music, however, follow a very different trajectory of sound. Here, the question about popular cultural form is not a question of its ultimate autonomy from the official culture – since that official culture is omnipresent – but how, against the single audible decibel level amplified at random with guns and tanks, popular music strikes its notes of difference.

The *words* of one of Cui Jian's most popular songs, 'Rock and Roll on the Road of the New Long March', allude to one of the founding heroic events of the Chinese communist state, the Long March to Yanan. The last few lines go as follows:

> What should I say, what should I do, in order to
>   be the real me
> How should I play, how should I sing, in
>   order to feel great
> I walk and think of snowy mountains and
>   grasslands
> I walk and sing of Chairman Mao
> Oh! one, two, three, four, five, six, seven.

By recalling the words, I don't mean to imply that the truth of Cui Jian's music lies in its verbal content. Rather, the disjuncturing of words from music points to the significance of the partial – of emotions as partializing rather than totalizing activities which jar with the symphonic effects of official culture.

There is, first of all, the difference between the 'decadence' of the music and the 'seriousness' of the subject matter to which the music alludes. Without knowing the 'language', we can dance to Cui Jian's song as we would to any rock-and-roll tune; once we pay attention to the words, we are in the solemn presence of history, with its insistence on emotional meaning and depth. This is why Cui Jian's music so deeply antagonized the officials in the Chinese state bureaucracy that he was dismissed from his post in the Beijing Symphony Orchestra and prohibited from performing in Beijing a couple of years ago. The official Chinese repudiation of his music is moralistic, aiming to reinforce a kind of obligatory cultural memory in which the founding deeds of communist ancestors are properly honoured instead of being 'played with' – least of all through the music imported from the capitalist West.

[...]

[...] In contemporary Chinese fiction, the forty years of communist history are increasingly understood to be the alienation of human life *par excellence* through what poses as the 'collective' good. The collective is now perceived as that mysterious, objectified Other against which one must struggle for one's life. Such is the instinctual battle fought by the protagonist in the controversial novel *Half of Man Is Woman* by Zhang Xianliang. Working in a labour camp in the countryside where official instructions are regularly announced through loudspeakers, this man reflects on physical labour in the following terms. Describing hard labour as a 'trance', he distinguishes between labour and the officially assigned 'job': 'A job is for someone else. Labour is your own.' This insistence on the difference between the work that is performed for a public sphere with clearly organized goals and the work that is one's own, is not an insistence on 'privacy' or private property, but rather a resistance against the coercive regimentation of emotions that is carried out under the massive collectivization of human lives in the Chinese communist state. Contrary to orthodox socialist beliefs, the protest made in contemporary Chinese popular culture is that such collectivization of human lives is what produces the deepest alienation ever because it turns human labour into the useful job that we are performing for that 'other' known as the collective, the country, the people, and so forth. [...]

At a time when we have become rightly alert to issues in the Third World, it is precisely the problem of 'use' that has to be rethought. Something is 'useful', we tend to think, because it serves a collective purpose. While on many occasions I have no objections to this kind of thinking, it is when we deal with the Third World that we have to be particularly careful in resorting to paradigms of the collective as such. Why? Such paradigms produce stereotypical views of members of Third World cultures, who are always seen as representatives driven solely by the cause of vindicating their own cultures. To the extent that such peoples are seen as representatives deprived of their individuality and

treated as members of a collective (read 'Third World') culture, I think that the morally supportive narrativizing of the Third World by way of utilitarianism, however sophisticatedly utilitarianism is argued, repeats what it tries to criticize, namely, the subjection of entire peoples to conceptual paradigms of life activities that may have little relevance to their struggles for survival.

In the case of China, I read the paradigm of collectivity as part of the legacy of imperialism imposed upon a 'backward' nation. Like most countries in the post-imperialist era, the alternative to ultimate destruction in the early twentieth century was, for the Chinese, to 'go collective' and produce a 'national culture'. Collectivity as such was therefore never an ethnic empowerment without neuroses, and it is the neuroses which are now surfacing in popular cultural forms like music. At this point in time, the narrative of collectivity does little to explain the kinds of emotions that are played (upon) in contemporary Chinese music, apart from making us notice this music's negativity and, for some, nihilism. These emotions of negativity suggest a deliberate turning away from the collective's thematic burdens through lightheartedness, sarcasm, and physicality.

[...]

Listening otherwise

The lyrics of the 'Song of the Dwarf' ('Zhuru zhi ge'), by the Taiwanese singer Luo Dayou, go as follows:

> We must hold hands, hold hands tight
> Beware of the giants waving at you from far away
> These history-making faces, these figures of the
>   time
> They are always carrying guns for the sake of the
>   people
>
> The road of the Long March is rough
> Forcing their way into Tiananmen, they
>   arrive at Beijing
> The index is alluring in the market of 'struggle'
> Revolutionary doctrines fluctuate like stock
>   prices
> Five thousand years of despotic rule await your
>   cleansing

Beware:

The characters who revolt against others are
    themselves revolted against

They clutch at their clothes. They need to have
    face.

How many lives has Mr. Marx destroyed

The glorious results of war are woven in our
    compatriots' blood

We dedicate the great victory to the people

Five thousands years of despotic rule await your
    cleansing

But who can wash the blood on your hands

We must hold hands, hold hands tight

Beware of the smile on the face of the dwarf who
    is approaching

These faces behind [him], these great figures –

They are always carrying guns for the sake of the
    people.

This song, once again, demonstrates that separation between musicality and verbality I mentioned as characteristic of many other songs. In the remarkable lines, 'the index is alluring in the market of "struggle"/Revolutionary doctrines fluctuate like stock prices', the mockery of the communist state is achieved by a clever combination of the languages of revolution and the market economy, or rather, by a rewriting of revolution in terms of the market economy, effecting a demolition of the altruistic claims made by the practitioners of the Marxist ideology, which is included as part of the 5000-year-old Chinese despotic tradition.

The clashing of the two usually incompatible languages, revolution and the market, suggests a fundamental need to revamp the bases for both. Their clashing reveals the grounding of emotions not in 'nature' but in technology. Because of the ineluctability of technology, what clash are also the thematics of the 'Third World' and the 'First World'. Technology is that collectivized goal to which East Asian cultures, as part of the non-Western world that survives in the backwash of imperialism, have no choice but to adopt. In the case of mainland China, the successful technologizing of an entire nation through the regimentation of life activities in collective form was accomplished through the communist revolution. In other, non-communist

Chinese communities in East Asia, notably Taiwan, Hong Kong and Singapore, the success of technology is evident in sophisticated modes of living, inseparable form the production and consumption of technology – the collectivized and the commodified – constitutes a unique type of ethnicity in ways that exceed the orthodox paradigms of demarcating First World and Third World economic and political networks.

Contrary to the paradigms of struggle and protest – the cultural stereotypes that are being laid across the Third World peoples with uniformity, soliciting them into a *coded* narrative whether or not they are willing to participate in it – the emotions that emerge here imply a new writing of ethnicity. This writing cannot consider the 'ethnic' person simply in the role of the oppressed whom we in the West, armed with questions such as 'Who speaks?', attempt to 'liberate' by giving a voice, a voice that amounts to a kind of waged labour (the permit to participate in the working world with 'choice' and freedom'). The presence of technology means that the deeply historical perception of the unpredictable but oppressive nature of official culture is here conveyed through instruments that are accomplices as well as resisters to that culture. Precisely because historical injustice is the very ground on which the struggle for injustice takes place, such injustice is the very ground on which the struggle for survival takes place, such injustice is often alluded to indirectly rather than confronted directly. The music of Cui Jian and Luo Dayou is as semantically loaded with the feelings of oppression as it is electronically saturated, but the feelings of oppression impinge upon us as an inerasable, *because* invisible, referent like a language with an insistent syntax but no obvious semiotics/signs with meanings.

Official Chinese culture, on the other hand, does not only suppress such *emotions* in order to uphold the glorious version of history; as usual, it would also criticize the *electronics* in the name of protecting the integrity of Chinese culture against excessive Westernization. Operating under the domination of a patriotic rhetoric that cannot be turned off, the counter-discourse we find in many popular songs is thus deliberately inarticulate, by way of a music that is lighthearted, decadent, playing to the rhythms of expensive lifestyles in forgetfulness of the wretched of the earth. The forms of nihilism are used consciously for enervation, producing moments of positivity that restructure relations to the political state.

[...]

'Hear there and everywhere': music miniaturized

What we need, in other words, is a history of listening – a history of how listening and how the emotions that are involved in listening change with the apparatuses that make listening possible. Traditionally, listening is, as a rule, public. For a piece of music to be heard – even under the most private circumstances – a certain public accessibility can always be assumed. Such public accessibility continues even when music becomes portable with the transistor radio and the portable cassette tape player. With the intervention of headphones, on the other hand, listening enters an era of interiorization whose effect of 'privacy' is made possible by the thoroughly mechanized nature of its operation. But listening through headphones is still attached to relatively large pieces of machinery, which tend to remain stationary. (We use them when we don't want to disturb others occupying the same space.)

The form of listening that is a decisive break from the past is that made possible by the Walkman. One critic describes the Walkman this way: 'that neat little object ... a pregnant zero, ... the unobstrusive link in an urban strategy, a semiotic shifter, the crucial digit in a particular organization of sense' (Chambers, 1990, p. 1). Even though the popular songs I am discussing may not be consciously intended for playing on the Walkman alone, what I would argue is that the conception of the Walkman is already written into these songs. The Walkman is implied in their composite mode of making, which corresponds to a composite mode of listening that involves multiple entries and exits, multiple turnings-on and turnings-off. If music is a kind of storage place for the emotions generated by cultural conflicts and struggles, then we can, with the new listening technology, talk about the production of such conflicts and struggles *on the human body* at the press of a button. In the age of the Walkman (or its more sophisticated affiliate, the Discman), the emotions have become portable.

In contrast to the gramophone or loudspeaker, without which the 'gigantic' history of the public would not have been possible, the Walkman ushers in the history of a miniaturized music. But the notion of miniature is useful here only indirectly, as a way to point to the need for us to invent another language that would more appropriately describe the partiality of music. Susan Stewart's study of the narratives of the miniature provides us with the necessary assistance. Among the most important characteristics of the miniature, according to Stewart, is that it establishes a correspondence with the things of which it is a miniature. The miniature is thus unimaginable without visuality: 'the miniature is a cultural product, the product of an eye performing certain operations, manipulating, and attending in certain ways to, the physical world' (Stewart, 1984, p. 55). The miniature is the labour of multiplying and intensifying significance microscopically: 'That the world of things can open itself to reveal a secret life – indeed, to reveal a set of actions and hence a narrativity and history outside the given field of perception – is a constant daydream that the miniature presents. This is a daydream of the microscope: the daydream of life inside life, of significance multiplied infinitely *within* significance' (p. 54; emphasis in original).

Insofar as Walkman music is shrunken music, music reduced to the size of the little portable machine that produces it, it is a kind of miniature. But the most important feature of music's miniaturization does not lie in the smallness of the equipment which generates it. Rather, it lies in the *revolution in listening* engendered by the equipment: while the music is hidden from others because it is compacted, this hiddenness is precisely what allows me to hear it full blast. The 'miniaturizing' that does not produce a visible body – however small – that corresponds with 'reality' leads to a certain freedom. This is the freedom to be deaf to the loudspeakers of history. We do not return to individualized or privatized emotions when we use the Walkman: rather the Walkman's artificiality makes us aware of the impending presence of the collective, which summons us with the infallibility of a sleepwalker. What the Walkman provides is the possibility of a barrier, a blockage between 'me' and the world, so that, as in moments of undisturbed sleep, I can disappear as a listener playing music. The Walkman allows me, in other words, to be missing – to be a missing part of history, to which I say: 'I am not there, not where you collect me'. In the Walkman, the hiding place for the music-operator, we find the music that, to borrow Attali's phrase, 'is to be produced everywhere it is possible to produce it ... by anyone who wants to enjoy it'. Here, Barthes' statement that 'Politics is not necessarily just talking, it can also be listening' takes on a new meaning. For listening is not, as Adorno describes popular music in America, 'a training course in ... passivity'; rather it is a 'silent' sabotage of the technology of collectivization with its own instruments.

As the machine of what we might call 'automatic playing', the Walkman offers a means of self-production in an age when any emphasis on individualist positions amounts to a scandal. What is scandalous is that self-production is now openly autistic. The autism of the Walkman listener irritates onlookers precisely because the onlookers find themselves reduced to the activity of looking alone. For once, voyeurism yields no secrets: one can look all one wants and still nothing is to be seen. The sight of the Walkman listener, much like the sight of some of our most brilliant scientists, artists, and theorists, is one that we cannot enter even with the most piercing glances. (The Walkman allows us for the first time to realize that our 'geniuses' have always lived with earphones on.) Critics of the Walkman, like critics of mass culture in general, are condemned to a position of exteriority, from which all kinds of ineffectual moralistic attacks are fired. This position of exteriority amounts to the charge: 'Look at yourself! Look how stupid you look!' But the autistic sigh is the one which is free of the responsibility to look, observe, and judge. Its existence does not depend on looking, especially not on looking at oneself.

The music operator's activity frankly reveals that the 'collective' is not necessarily an 'other' to be idealized from afar, but a mundane, mechanical, portable *part* of ourselves which can be tucked away in our pocket and called up at will. This 'self' production through the collective requires not so much slogans as it does AA batteries, and it takes place in the midst of other, perhaps equally significant, activities. It substitutes listening for the writing of music and demolishes the myth of creativity through a composite discoursing of the emotions. The noises and voices of production become ingredients of self-making. Deprived of their images and their bodily presence in on-stage performances, even singers – 'stars' and 'icons' – become part of the technologically exteriorized 'inner speech' of the listener. As such, the emotions of music are dehydrated, condensed, and encapsulated, so that they can be carried from place to place and played instantly – at 'self-service'.

References

CHAMBERS, I. (1990) 'A miniature history of the Walkman', *New Formations: a journal of culture/theory/politics*, No. 11, pp. 1–4.

STEWART, S. (1984) *On Longing: narratives of the miniature, the gigantic, the souvenir, the collection*, Baltimore, MD, Johns Hopkins University Press.

Source: Chow, 1993, pp. 385–8, 391–2, 394–6, 396–9.

READING G
Iain Chambers: 'A miniature history of the Walkman'

[…] Could it be that we come to the city in order to achieve solitude? Such has been the unspoken premise of the modern city of utopian individualism. By solitude I do not mean isolation. Isolation is a state of nature; solitude is the work of culture. Isolation is an imposition, solitude a choice. (Hatton, 1988)

1990 is the tenth anniversary of the Sony Walkman. Launched in the Spring of 1980, this urban, hi-fi gadget was based on an idea that came to Akio Morita, President of Sony, while, rather appropriately, walking in New York. Over the decade the Walkman has offered access to a portable soundtrack which, unlike the transistor radio, car stereo and the explicitly opposed intention of the bass-boosted 'ghetto blaster' or 'boogie box', is, above all, an intensely private experience. But such an apparent refusal of public exchange and regression to individual solitude also involves an unsuspected series of extensions. With the Walkman there is simultaneously a concentration of the auditory environment and an extension of our individual bodies.

For the meaning of the Walkman does not necessary lie in itself – it sits there, neat, usually black, often wrapped in leather, and quite oblivious – but in the extension of perceptive potential. Although people walking around with a Walkman might simply seem to signify a void, the emptiness of metropolitan life and its 'streets without memory' (Siegfried Kracauer), that neat little object can also be understood as a pregnant zero, as the unobtrusive link in an urban strategy, a semiotic shifter, the crucial digit in a particular organization of sense […]

In the apparent refusal of sociability the Walkman act nevertheless reaffirms participation in a shared environment. It directly partakes in the changes in the horizon of perception that characterize the late twentieth century, and which offers a world fragmenting under the mounting media accumulation of intersecting signs, sounds and images. With the Walkman strapped to our bodies we confront what Murray Schafer in his book *The Tuning of the World* calls a 'soundscape', a soundscape that increasingly represents a mutable collage: sounds are selected, sampled, folded in and cut up by both the producers (DJs, rap crews, dub masters, recording engineers) and the consumers (we put together our personal play lists, skip some tracks, repeat others, turn up the volume to block out the external soundtrack or flip between the two). Each listener/player selects and rearranges the soundtrack or flip soundscape, and, in constructing a dialogue with it, leaves a trace in the network.

In this mobile, wraparound world, the Walkman, like dark glasses and iconoclastic fashion, serves to set one apart while simultaneously reaffirming individual contact to certain common, if shifting, measures (music, fashion, aesthetics, metropolitan life … and their particular cycles of mortality). So the Walkman is both a mask and a masque: a quiet putting into act of localized theatrics. It reveals itself as a significant symbolic gadget for the nomads of modernity, in which music on the move is continually being decontextualized and recontextualized in the inclusive acoustic and symbolic life of everyday life (Hosokawa, 1984)[1]. But if the Walkman so far represents the ultimate form of music on the move, it also represents the ultimate musical means in mediating the media. For it permits the possibility, however fragile and however transitory, of imposing your soundscape on the surrounding aural environment and thereby domesticating the external world: for a moment it can all be brought under the stop/start, fast forward, pause and rewind buttons.

The fascination of the image of the Walkman, apart from the inner secret it brazenly displays in public (what is s/he listening to?), is the ambiguous position that it occupies between autism and autonomy: that mixture of danger and saving power, to paraphrase Heidegger's quotation from Hölderlin[2], that characterizes modern technology. Therefore, to understand the Walkman both involves multiplying on it diverse points of view and appreciating that it does not subtract from sense but adds to and complicates it. Pursuing this we might say that our relationship to the Walkman 'will be free if it opens our human existence to the essence of technology' (Heidegger, 1977, p. 3). By 'essence' (*Wesen*) Heidegger intends something that endures through time, that dwells in the present, that offers a 'sense' of technology that is not merely reducible to the 'technological'. Despite the nostalgia for authenticity that hangs over Heidegger's discourse we can perhaps bend his words in a suggestive direction. To the question what is technology and, in this particular case, the Walkman, we can answer that it is simultaneously a means and a cultural activity. To continue with the German philosopher's concerns, the Walkman is an instrument and activity that contributes to the casting into, or en-framing (*Ge-stell*), of sense in the contemporary world. In retracing the etymology of 'technology' back to the Greek *techne* and its ancient connection to the arts, to *poiesis* and knowledge, Heidegger suggests a means of revealing its sense, its particular truth.

But as both instrument and activity, the Walkman is not simply an instrument that reveals the enduring truth of technology and being; it is also an immediate reality and activity. As part of the equipment of modern nomadism it contributes to the prosthetic extension of our bodies, perpetually 'on the move', caught up in a decentred diffusion of languages, experiences, identities, idiolects and histories that are distributed in a tendentially global syntax. The Walkman encourages us to think inside this new organization of time and space. Here, for example, the older, geometrical model of the city as the organizer of space has increasingly being replaced by chronometry and the organization of time. The technology of space has been supplemented and increasingly eroded by the technology of time: the 'real time', the 'nanoseconds' of computer chips and monitor blips, of transitory information on a screen, of sounds snatched in the headphones. It leads to the emergence of a further dimension. 'Speed suddenly returns to become a *primitive force* beyond the measure of both time and space' (Virilo, 1988, p. 15; see also Virilo, 1984).

To travel, and to perform our *travail*, in this environment we plug in, choosing a circuit. Here, as opposed to the discarded 'grand narratives' (Lyotard) of the city, the Walkman offers the possibility of a micro-narrative, a customized story and soundtrack. The ingression of such a privatized habitat in public spaces is a disturbing act. Its uncanny quality lies in its deliberate confusion of earlier boundaries, in its provocative appearance 'out of place'. Now, the confusion of 'place', of voices, histories and experiences speaking 'out of place', forms part of the altogether more extensive sense of contemporary semantic and political crisis. [For a further discussion of the politics of 'place', see Chambers, 1990.] A previous order and organization of place, and their respective discourses, has had increasingly to confront an excess of languages emerging out of the histories and languages of feminism, sexual rights, ethnicity, race, and the environment, that overflow and undercut its authority. Is the Walkman therefore a political act? It is certainly an act that unconsciously entwines with many other micro-activities in conferring a different sense on the *polis*. In producing a different sense of space and time, it participates in rewriting the conditions of representation: where 'representation' clearly indicates both the iconic or semiotic dimension of the everyday *and* potential participation in a political community.

In Bruce Chatwin's marvellous book *The Songlines* we are presented with the idea that the world was initially sung into being.

> I have a vision of the Songlines stretching across the continents and ages; that wherever men have trodden they have left a trail of song (of which we may, now and then, catch an echo); and that these trails must reach back, in time and space, to an isolated pocket in the African savannah, where the First Man opening his mouth in defiance of the terrors that surrounded him, shouted the opening stanza of the World Song, 'I AM!'. (Chatwin, 1988, p. 314)

The Nietzschian vision of the world, that is a world of our making, dependent on our activity and language for its existence, is here laid out as a the human adventure in which the movements of peoples and the rigours and rhythms of bodies, limbs and voice set the patterns, the design, the nomination, of the land, the country, our home. The religious aura of this physical and sonorial nomadism has clearly waned in the more secular networks of Western society. Perhaps it still continues to echo inside the miniaturized headphones of modern nomads as the barely remembered traces of a once sacred journey intent on celebrating its presence in a mark, voice, sign, symbol, signature, to be left along the track.

Notes

1   This is a brilliant, pioneering essay on the question of the Walkman. It is extracted from a full-length study in Japanese: Shuhei Hosokawa, *Walkman no Shûjigaku* (Tokyo: 1981).

2   The lines from Friedrich Hölderlin's poem 'Patmos' are:

> But where danger is, grows
>
> The saving power also.

References

CHAMBERS, I. (1990) *Border Dialogues: journeys in postmodernity*, Routledge, London and New York.

CHATWIN, B. (1988) *The Songlines*, Cape, London.

HATTON, B. (1988) 'From neurosis to narrative', in *Metropolis: new British architecture and the city*, London.

HEIDEGGER, M. (1977) 'The question concerning technology' in Heidegger, M. (1977) *The Question Concerning Technology and Other Essays*, New York, Harper & Row.

HOSOKAWA, S. (1984) 'The Walkman effect', *Popular Music*, 4 , pp. 171–3.

SCHAFER, R. MURRAY (1977) *The Tuning of the World*, New York, Knopf.

VIRILO, P. (1984) *L'espace critique*, Paris.

VIRILO, P. (1988) *Lo spazio critico,* Bari.

Source: Chambers, 1990, pp. 1–4.

READING H
Vincent Jackson: 'Menace II society'

> 'Wear a Walkman and you're travelling strapped. A Menace to Society.'

As anyone who travels on the London Underground knows, each trip is full of grief. No matter how long or short your journey, you can always guarantee that at some point on your journey, someone or something will piss you off. Crowded carriages when it always seems to be your nose that is stuffed into the armpit of the person with BO. Dirty unshaven buskers who cannot sing, playing jolly folk music (and who also have BO). The endless hours spent in tunnels due to the ubiquitous 'security alert'.

Alright. These are things I can just about bear. But there is one thing that tops all of this, that makes my blood boil, makes me want to go psycho like Norman Bates. Eyes. Dirty looks. Cold stares.

You get on the train. You sit down. You get bored looking at the sad faces around you. You reach into your bag. You pull out your Walkman. You stick in your tape [...] You press the play button. BAM! The Eyes. Icy glares tell it all. In the short time it takes for the other passengers to look you up and down with utter contempt, you have already had a huge label slapped across your forehead. You are a scumbag, a low-life, a loser. For some strange reason, the Walkman has become the scourge of the modern day traveller, the leper's bell, symbolic of the endemic rebellion in today's youth culture. Wear a Walkman and you're travelling strapped. A Menace to Society.

In my experience, nine times out of ten, the owners of the stony stares are suit-wearers. This is the type of guy who, because he is wearing a £100 Burton outfit and earns £10,000 a year making irrelevant videos for a city insurance firm, is suddenly of the opinion that he is The Man.

Now don't get me wrong. I've got absolutely nothing against suit wearers. Yet it must be said that these are the same people who, on a jam-packed carriage at 8am, when it is impossible to move an inch, insist on reading their Daily Telegraph despite the fact that it is being shoved halfway up your nostrils. But hey, do I complain? It may seem ludicrous that people moan about the barely perceptible sound of a

Walkman while travelling on a 200 ton train that jolts around violently enough to measure on the Richter scale, but like most things in life, the problem goes much deeper than it appears on the surface. It's not the sound coming out of your headphones that bothers people around you, it's the symbolism.

The device is, in most cases, worn by young people. These are the same young people who are widely perceived as being losers, dole-scrounger and drug-takers. When your average commuter spots a young person casually dressed (military boots, baggy jeans, hat) nodding his or her head to the beat of the Walkman, they immediately connect the personal stereo to all that represents the insubordination of youth.

The experience of listening to your Walkman is intensely insular. It signals a desire to cut yourself off from the rest of the world at the touch of a button. You close your eyes and you could be anywhere. You can be a rapper, a deejay, dancer. Hell, when you put on that tape and drift away, you could be a superstar.

The problem is though, society is extremely wary of people who want to disengage themselves from the rest of the world. Those who do not wish to join in. Play your Walkman and you might as well shout 'Everybody just piss off!' No wonder we get the Eyes. The damned Eyes. So much for my theory. But being the type of person who likes to back up what I say, I decided to conduct some in-depth scientific research. So, armed only with my Walkman, a clipboard and a slide rule I got on the District Line at Southfields. The few bods sitting opposite me minding their own business became my subjects. Moving slowly so as not to alarm them I reached into my bag and pulled out my Walkman. Observation revealed that subjects had begun to look decidedly edgy. Then, with the creeping growing of satisfaction that a man get when he can feel he is about to be proved right, I put the headphones on and pressed the play button. BAM! My bets for the first dirty look were placed firmly on the balding guy in the cheap suit – but no! He was pipped at the post by a middle aged librarian type woman who gave me The Eyes a mere two seconds after the play button had clicked. She looked me up and down in the same contemptuous manner I had received thousands of times before during many

years of Walkman wearing. The Eyes said it all. SCUMBAG! LOW-LIFE! LOSER!

But wait. There's a cunning twist to my tale. The punchline to the story is this, people. When I pressed the play button *there wasn't even a cassette in the machine!*

As I stepped off the train at Embankment and headed towards Soho for some serious record shopping, it occurred to me that the public's loathing of the Walkman has a lot to do with the British disease of resenting other people's enjoyment. This malaise is evident through all echelons of British society; through the legal system that prevents us from getting a drink after 11pm, a government that wants to enact a Criminal Justice Bill to stop us dancing to our 'repetitive beats', down to the average bod in the street who can't stand the sight of a person enjoying themselves listing to a pair of headphones. Watch the looks of disgust when a couple kiss on the underground. Or even when someone laughs. Watch the strange looks that person receives, the looks that say 'What a nutter'.

And now the price of playing your Walkman in public can be even higher than a few dirty looks. Just as Andrew Dunn, a 21 year old student from Thirsk, North Yorkshire, who was fined £300 after a passenger on a British Rail train from Leeds to York complained that his Walkman was too loud. The music that was supposedly booming out of his headphones was middle of the road pop group Beautiful South. Just imagine if the bass heavy beats of Erick Sermon, KRS 1, Buju Banton or General Levy had been blasting out. What would the find have been then? £1,000? £10,000? A public flogging? Death row? Let's put this ridiculous fine into perspective. Remember the guy on the news recently who suffered the ultimate shame when a security screen trapped him by the neck as he tried to retrieve a stolen credit card at a petrol station? Well he was sentenced to 100 hours community service. If you assume that the menial work that he'll be doing would probably be valued at around £3 an hour on the free market, then his crime is equal to Andrew Dunn's in the eyes of the law. Just another example of how [mixed] up British justice is.

So to all you homeboys, homegirls, house heads, reggae fans, soul boys, techno freaks and music lovers in general. The next time you are on the tube, listening to your Walkman, trying to put up with the three Bs (BOs, Busking and Bombs), and some fool looks at you as if you are pond life, please try not to get angry. I know it is tempting to go up and punch them in the face for their narrow mindedness, but hey – we are civilised intelligent young people who do not need to resort to such football hooligan tactics. Just chill out, smile and turn up the volume. But damn those Eyes, those bloody Eyes.

Source: Jackson, 1994, pp. 15–17.

Acknowledgements

Grateful acknowledgement is made to the following sources for permission to reproduce material in this book:

Text

p. 117: Melody Maker, 17 September 1994*;*
Reading A: Excerpts from 'The work of art in the age of mechanical reproduction' in *Illuminations* by Walter Benjamin, copyright © 1955 by Suhrkamp Verlag, Frankfurt a.M., English translation by Harry Zohn copyright © 1968 and renewed by Harcourt Brace and Company, reprinted by permission of the publisher. Also by permission of Harvard University Press; *Reading B:* Williams, R. (1983) *Towards 2000*, Chatto and Windus, from *Towards 2000* by Raymond Williams. Copyright © 1983 by Raymond Williams. Reprinted by permission of Pantheon Books, a division of Random House, Inc.; *Reading C:* Lyons, N. (1976) *The Sony Vision*, Crown Publishers, Inc., by permission of Sony Corporation of America; *Reading D:* Shu Ueyama (1982) 'The selling of the "Walkman"', *Advertising Age*, 22 March 1982, Crain Communications, Inc; *Reading E:* Harvey, T. A. (1988) 'How Sony Corporation became first with kids', *Adweek's Marketing Week*, 21 November 1988, ASM Communications, Inc.; *Reading F:* Chow, R. (1990) 'Listening otherwise, music miniaturized: a different type of question about revolution', *Discourse*, Vol. 13, No. 1, Winter 1990/91, © 1990 Rey Chow; *Reading G:* Chambers, I. (1990) 'A miniature history of the Walkman', *New Formations*, No. 11, Routledge; *Reading H:* Jackson, V. (1994) 'Menace II society', *Touch Magazine*, Vol. 42, November 1994.

Figures

Figures 1.1, 1.2, 1.6, 3.1, 3.2, 3.3, 3.7: Sony UK Ltd*;* *Figures 1.4, 1.5, 1.9, 1.17:* Grateful thanks to CCP Positioning, Milan; *Figures 1.7 and 1.8:* Advertising Archives; *Figures 1.3,1.10, 1.11, 1.12, 1.13:* Sony UK Ltd. and Bartle Bogle Hegarty; *Figure 1.14:* Sony Corporation, from *Advertising Age*, 22 March 1982*;* *Figure 1.15:* Copyright Uli Rose, Rose Photo Inc, New York; *Figure 1.16:* *Marketing and Media Decisions*, October 1981; *Figure 2.1:* Kurita/Gamma/ Frank Spooner Pictures; *Figure 2.2:* Ashley Ashwood/Financial Times Pictures; *Figures 2.3, 3.6:* Sony Corporation; *Figure 3.4:* Japan Information and Cultural Centre, London; *Figure 3.5:* Radio Corporation of America; *Figure 5.1:* Adapted from *Mintel Marketing Report*, June 1992, Courtesy of MINTEL/BMRB; *Figure 5.2:* McCann-Erickson Agency, taken from *Advertising Age*, 30 March 1981, p. 3.

Photographs

p.7: Rupert Heath; *p. 61:* Sonya Hutchison; *p. 83:* Grant Auger; *p. 91:* Greg Saturley and Simon Turner; *pp. 75, 93, 94, 107 (all):* © James Mollison; *p. 96:* Paul Antick/Jessica Evans; *p. 133:* R. Khurana; *p. 117:* Courtesy of the London Transport Museum.

Table

Table 5.1: Adapted from *Mintel Marketing Report*, June 1992, Courtesy of MINTEL/BMRB.

Index